DECORATED CAKES

by
Mary Ford

WITH STEP-BY-STEP INSTRUCTIONS

Printed and bound in Great Britain by Purnell Book Productions Ltd.

ISBN 0 946429 04 9

All cake designs in this book have been previously published in either Mary Ford's 101 Cake Designs or Mary Ford's Cake Designs - Another 101

The Authors.

Mary was born in Wick Village, near Bristol. Her interest in cake icing started when her father, a flour miller, encouraged her to take up the craft.

On leaving school, therefore, Mary went straight into a bakery on a four-year apprenticeship, with a day release each week to attend a course at Bristol Technical College, where she gained her Final City and Guilds in Bread Making and Flour Confectionery.

Having moved to London to gain greater experience, Mary finally settled in Bournemouth where she started teaching cake icing in Bournemouth and Southampton Colleges. That eventually led to private tuition.

She met and married Michael and as their business increased, so ever larger premises were found to accommodate larger classes. Mary, throughout this period, continued icing cakes to order and instructing students who were arriving from all parts of the World.

Mary makes no secret of the fact that cake decoration is the consuming passion of her life. She has won innumerable awards in the craft.

Michael was born in Croydon, Surrey. His ambition to succeed in the culinary arts began at school, where he was the only boy to study cookery. This led to a three-year course in bread making and flour confectionery at Plymouth Technical College. There Michael achieved the Final City and Guilds in the subject.

He then travelled the country to further his practical experience in various hotels, restaurants and bakeries. He visited Bournemouth to work in a bakery and there met and married Mary in 1970.

His ambition to manage his own business came to fruition 12 months later when, with Mary, he created the forerunner to the Mary Ford Cake Artistry Centre.

Michael introduced a number of ideas in order to expand the company, including mail order, correspondence courses throughout the World and the development and manufacture of cake artistry tools.

A natural follow-up to the correspondence courses was the production of books on cake icing artistry for which Michael has been responsible for all the photography.

Preface

Over many years our friends and customers asked us to produce a cake icing book and this we did in 1982. That book 101 Cake Designs - proved to be a best seller and created the demand for a second book. The challenge became irresistible to us and the result was Mary Ford's Cake Designs - Another 101.

By demand, we are now producing this series of titles devoted to specialist types of cakes, selected from our first two books.

We sincerely trust this book, as well as its companion books, will give much pleasure and help to all who use them in the pursuit of excellence in cake icing artistry.

Our thanks go to Stan and Betty Oddy and all who have helped in the preparation of this book.

Michael and Mary

Introduction

The Mary Ford Story is a fairy tale come true. No waving of a magic wand has however brought about the success and quality of product which is associated with the Mary Ford Cake Artistry Centre. Hard work, dedication, perseverence and consistently high standards of product have achieved this.

Michael and Mary Ford manage their enterprise from premises in Southbourne, Bournemouth, England. From this base they bake and sell their own bread and confectionary; ice celebratory cakes to order and give, amongst other things, instruction in cake icing as well as bread, pastry, cake and chocolate making. Demonstrations in the art of cake icing are featured and the Cake Artistry Centre sells, by mail order and over the counter, all manner of cake icing equipment, decorations and raw materials.

All this is a long way from the one small room in an hotel annexe where, in 1971, Mary commenced instructing just six pupils each session. Michael and Mary progressed to their first retail outlet and then moved to their present address. To raise part of the capital they then needed, their home had to be sold - such was the faith in their own ability and urge to succeed.

The quality of the Mary Ford Centre work is a byword to professionals and amateurs alike and this book, is the latest in a comprehensive list of outstanding goods to come from Mary Ford and, as is only to be expected, is produced in a highly professional and, thus, easy to follow manner.

For years now the British have led the world in cake icing artistry - especially in the use of royal icing - and our pre-eminence in this field is due solely to the skills of craftspeople like England's Mary Ford. She is an undoubted world leader in her chosen profession and, through her books on step-by-step icing instructions, has received a well earned international recognition and reputation.

To answer a growing demand for cake icing books on different subjects Mary has specially selected twenty-seven decorated cake designs from her two best selling books:

Mary Ford 101 Cake Designs

Mary Ford's Cake Designs - Another 101

Without fear of contradiction, it can be said that this beautifully produced book - containing almost 1000 coloured photographs - is a work of art in its own right. For, each of the twenty-seven cake designs featured in the book, enjoys a full-page colour photograph and every stage of each design is pictured in thirty-two step-by-step coloured photographs and supported by easy to follow written instructions.

Other books in the series:

Novelty Cakes
Birthday Cakes
Wedding Cakes

These are outstanding books which both professional and amateur will value owning.

S & B

Contents

Reference table to cake designs.

NAME	OCCASION	STYLE	PAGES	FRUIT CAKE SIZES (inches)	SPONGE CAKE SIZES (inches)	BOARD SIZES (inches)	MARZIPAN (lbs)	ROYAL ICING (lbs)	SUGAR PASTE (lbs)	BUTTER CREAM (lbs)
ANDREW	Christening	square (cot)	84-86	9	-	12	2½	3½	-	-
BOBBIE	Christmas	round	42-44	8	-	11	1½	2	-	-
CATHRYN	Christening	square/round	75-77	10, 6	-	13, 6*	4	5	-	-
CLAIRE	Engagement	heart	93-95	8	-	11	2	3	-	-
COURTNEY	Retirement	crossword	78-80	9	-	12	2½	2	2	-
ERNIE	Retirement	chair	90-92	-	2 @ 10" sq.	14	-	½	1½	1
FELICITY	Confirmation	Bible	81-83	8	-	14	2	3	½	-
GEORGIANA	Welcome home	round	33-35	8	-	11	1½	2	-	-
HARVEY	Welcome home	square	24-26	8	-	11	2	2½	-	-
JACQUI	Wedding	2 tier square	57-59	10, 7	-	14, 10	4½	5½	-	-
JANET	Wedding	4 tier square	45-47	11, 9, 7, 5	-	15, 12, 10, 8	9	9	-	-
JOYCE	Christmas	square	39-41	7	-	10	1½	1½	-	-
KAY	Wedding	1 tier square	60-62	9	-	12	2½	3	-	-
MARK	Confirmation	round	15-17	8	-	11	1½	2	-	-
MEMORY	Memorial	oval	18-20	9	-	12	2	2	½	-
MERRIE	Christmas	round	36-38	8	-	11	1½	2½	-	-
PAMELA	Engagement	round/heart	72-74	12, 6	-	15, (10)	4½	5	-	-
PAULA	Wedding	2 tier hexagonal	51-53	10, 7	-	13, 10	3½	3½	-	-
PEDRO	Holiday	sombrero	30-32	2 pt basin	-	16	1	3½	-	-
PETER	Father's Day	river fishing	69-71	8	-	11	2	3	½	-
RAYMOND	Congratulations	1st prize	27-29	8	-	11	2	2	½	-
ROSETTA	Wedding	3 tier round	63-65	10, 8, 6	-	16, 13, 8*, 6*	5	5	3	-
SALLY	Engagement	square	21-23	9	-	13	2½	3½	-	-
SANDRA	Wedding	1 tier round	48-50	8	-	13, 11	1½	3	-	-
SERENA	Wedding	4 tier round	54-56	12, 9, 6, 4	-	16, 9*, 6*, 4*	7	8	-	-
SYLVIA	Anniversary	square	87-89	8	-	11	2	3	½	-
TREVOR	Retirement	clock	66-68	-	2 @ 9" rd	12	-	1	1½	½

* Thin cake card.

This reference table is a guide to the materials used to produce the actual cakes featured in this book. You can, of course, choose whatever material quantities and sizes you wish. Refer to the main photograph in each instance for the appropriate shape of board and cake.

N.B. STRONGER COLOURS HAVE BEEN USED IN THE PREPARATION OF THE STEP-BY-STEP PHOTOGRAPHS IN THIS BOOK TO ACHIEVE CLARITY OF DEFINITION. NATURALLY, ANY COLOUR CHOICE IS YOURS

Basic Cake Recipe

Imperial/Metric	American
2 oz/57 g plain flour	½ cup all purpose flour
2 oz/57 g brown sugar	⅓ cup brown sugar
2 oz/57 g butter	¼ cup butter
2½ oz/71 g currants	½ cup currants
2½ oz/71 g sultanas	½ cup seedless white raisins
1 oz/28 g seedless raisins	3 tablespoons seedless raisins
1 oz/28 g glacé cherries	3 tablespoons candied cherries
1½ oz/42 g mixed peel	4½ tablespoons candied peel
¾ oz/21 g ground almonds	2½ tablespoons ground almonds
½ fluid oz/2 teaspoons brandy or rum	2 teaspoons brandy or rum
1 large egg	1 large egg
pinch nutmeg	pinch nutmeg
pinch mixed spice	pinch apple pie spice
pinch salt	pinch salt
¼ lemon zest and juice	¼ lemon zest and juice

Preparation. First line your tin with a double layer of buttered greaseproof paper. Then clean and prepare the fruit, halve the cherries. Mix all fruit together with lemon zest. Sift flour, spices and salt.
Method. Beat the butter until light. Add sugar to butter and beat again until light. Gradually add egg, beating in thoroughly after each addition. Stir in ground almonds. Fold in flour and spices. Finally add fruit together with brandy or rum and lemon juice. Mix well together and transfer to tin.

It is most important to follow the exact measurements and mixture of the foregoing ingredients.

In baking the cake initially, if one pint of water is placed in a meat tray in the bottom of the oven, this will create sufficient humidity to keep the top of the cake moist and ensure level results in baking. Remove water after half baking time.

When the cake is baked, leave it in the tin (pan) for one day, remove from tin (pan) then sprinkle the appropriate quantity of soaking mixture. Wrap cake in waxed paper and leave in a cupboard for three weeks. When the waxed paper becomes sticky, this means that moisture is seeping out, a sure sign that the cake is mature. If more liquid is required, add just before marzipanning. A cake needs no more than three weeks to mature.

CAKE PORTIONS: TO CALCULATE SIZE OF FRUIT CAKE REQUIRED 8 PORTIONS ARE GENERALLY CUT FROM EACH 1 LB OF FINISHED ICED CAKE.
Soaking mixture. Equal quantities of Rum, Sherry and Glycerine or spirits of choice. 1 tbls. per 1 lb of cake when required.

Glycerine – Table for use

For soft-cutting icing (per 1 lb or 454 g or 3½ cups of ready-made Royal Icing) use 1 teaspoon of glycerine for the bottom tier of a 3-tier wedding cake.
2 teaspoons of glycerine for the middle tier.
3 teaspoons of glycerine for the top tier, or for single tier cakes.
(N.B. Glycerine only to be added after Royal Icing has been made.)
NO GLYCERINE IN ROYAL ICING FOR RUNOUTS OR No. 1 WORK.

Royal Icing Recipe

Imperial/Metric
1½ ozs/42 g powdered egg white
½ pint/284 ml cold water
3½ lb/1½ kg best icing sugar sieved

OR

½ oz/14 g powdered egg white
3 fluid ozs/3 tablespoons cold water
1 lb/454 g best icing sugar, sieved

OR

3 egg whites (separated the day before)
1 lb/454 g best icing sugar (approximately) sieved

American
¼ cup powdered egg white + 2 tablespoons
1¼ cups cold water
3½ cups confectioner's sugar sifted

OR

¼ cup powdered egg white
3 tablespoons cold water
3½ cups confectioner's sugar, sifted

OR

3 egg whites (separated the day before)
3½ cups confectioner's sugar (approximately) sifted

Preparation. All equipment used must be perfectly cleaned and sterilised. Pour water into a jug and stir in powdered egg white. This will go lumpy and necessitates standing the mixture for one hour, stirring occasionally. Then strain through a muslin.

Method. Pour solution or egg whites into a mixing bowl and place the icing sugar on top. A drop of blue colour (color) may be added for white icing. Beat on slow speed for approximately 15-20 minutes or until the right consistency is obtained. (If powdered egg white is used the Royal Icing will keep in good condition for 2 weeks. Fresh egg whites will deteriorate quicker). Store Royal Icing in sealed container in a cool place.

Buttercream
(Referred to as CREAM in the Book)

Imperial/Metric
4 ozs/113 g butter
6-8 ozs/170-227 g icing sugar
1-2 tablespoons warm water
essence or flavouring of choice

American
½ cup butter
1⅓-2 cups confectioner's sugar
1-2 tablespoons warm water
extract or flavouring of choice

Method. Sift icing sugar. Soften butter and beat until light. Gradually add the icing sugar beating well after each addition. Add essence (extract) or flavouring (flavoring) of choice and water (carefully).

Heavy Genoese Sponge Recipe

Imperial/Metric
3 oz/85 g butter
3 oz/85 g margarine
6 oz/170 g caster sugar
3 eggs, lightly beaten
6 oz/170 g self-raising flour sieved

American
6 tablespoons butter
6 tablespoons margarine
¾ cup sugar
3 eggs, lightly beaten
1½ cups self-raising flour sifted

Preparation. First line your tin (pans) with greased greaseproof paper.

Method. Cream butter and margarine. Add sugar and beat until light in colour and fluffy in texture. Add the egg a little at a time beating after each addition. Carefully fold in the flour.
Bake: 190°C, 375°F, Gas 5. 20-25 minutes.

½ recipe makes 1 @ 8″ Rd sponge
or 1 @ 7″ Sq
1 recipe makes 1 @ 10″ Rd sponge
or 1 @ 9″ Sq
1½ recipe makes 1 @ 12″ Rd sponge
or 1 @ 11″ Sq

Sugar Paste Recipe
(Cold Fondant Recipe)

Imperial/Metric
1 lb/454 g icing sugar, sieved
1 egg white
2 ozs/57 g liquid glucose (Slightly warmed)

American
3½ cups Confectioner's sugar, sifted
1 egg white
4 tablespoons liquid glucose (Slightly warmed)

Method. Add egg white and glucose to icing sugar. Blend all ingredients together. Knead well until a smooth paste is obtained.
Keep in a polythene bag or sealed container and in a cool place. Colour and flavour (flavor) as required.

CONVERSION TABLES

WEIGHT		SIZE	
IMPERIAL	METRIC	IMPERIAL	METRIC
½ oz	14 g	5 ins	12.5 cm
1 oz	28 g	6 ins	15 cm
2 oz	57 g	7 ins	18 cm
3 oz	85 g	8 ins	20.5 cm
4 oz	113 g	9 ins	23 cm
5 oz	142 g	10 ins	25.5 cm
6 oz	170 g	11 ins	28 cm
7 oz	198 g	12 ins	30.5 cm
8 oz	227 g	13 ins	33 cm
9 oz	255 g	14 ins	35.5 cm
10 oz	284 g	15 ins	38 cm
11 oz	312 g	16 ins	40.5 cm
12 oz	340 g		
13 oz	369 g		
14 oz	397 g		
15 oz	425 g		
16 oz	454 g		

	LIQUID		
IMPERIAL	METRIC		AMERICAN
1 tsp.	5 ml		1 tsp
1 tbsp	15 ml		1 tbsp
1 fl.oz	28 ml		⅛ cup
2 fl. oz	57 ml		¼ cup
3 fl. oz	85 ml		⅜ cup
4 fl. oz	113 ml		½ cup
¼ pint	142 ml		⅝ cup
½ pint	284 ml		1¼ cup
1 pint	568 ml		2½ cup

Note: AUSTRALIAN TABLESPOON
4 tsp. 20ml 1 tbsp (AUS)

CAKE SIZES AND QUANTITIES WITH APPROXIMATE BAKING TIMES
(QUANTITIES ARE STATED IN MULTIPLES OF EACH OF THE BASIC RECIPES)

	Basic Fruit Cake Recipe (Bake at 275°F, 140°C, Gas Mark 1)						Heavy Genoese Sponge Recipe (Bake at 375°F, 190°C, Gas Mark 5)		
SIZE ins	ROUND	SQUARE	HORSE SHOE	HEART	HEXAGONAL	APPROX TIMING	ROUND	SQUARE	APPROX TIMING
5	1	1½	-	1½	1	1½-1¾ hrs	-	-	-
6	1½	2	1¼	2	1½	1¾-2 hrs	-	-	-
7	2	3	-	3	2	2½-3 hrs	-	½	20-25 mins
8	3	4	2½	4	3	3½-4 hrs	½	-	20-25 mins
9	4	5	-	5	4	4-4½ hrs	-	1	20-25 mins
10	5	6	4½	6	5	4¼-4¾ hrs	1	-	25-30 mins
11	6	7	-	7	6	4½-5 hrs	-	1½	25-30 mins
12	7	8	6½	8	7	5-5½ hrs	1½	-	25-30 mins

Template graph and instructions.

(Do not remove or draw directly onto this graph.)

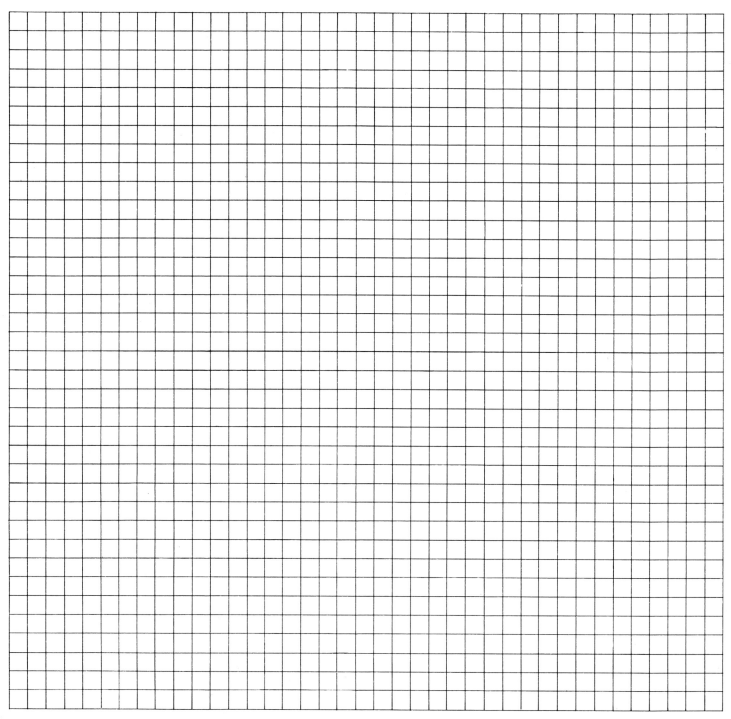

Explanatory note:
Most cakes in this book include artwork necessitating the use of graphs (for an example please refer to the drawing of the cross template in picture No.2 of the cake 'Mark' on page 16). All graphs, such as that in picture No.2, need to be adjusted to obtain the correct scale. this can be achieved by using the following instructions.

Instructions:
1. Count and record the number of squares in picture No.2.
2. Cover the TEMPLATE GRAPH with a sheet of greaseproof paper and count out, mark and trace the equivalent number of squares on the greaseproof paper.
3. Remove the greaseproof paper graph and return to page 16.

4. Wherever the drawings in picture No.2 crosses a line, mark the identical crossing point on the greaseproof paper graph.
5. Still using the picture as a guide, join the marks on the greaseproof paper graph to re-create drawing No.2 on page 16.

Equipment.

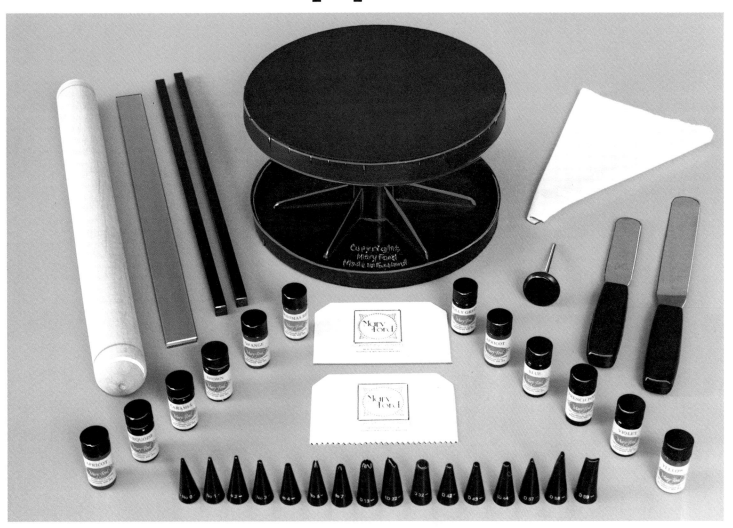

Turntable	Straight edge	Plain scraper	Flower nail
6" Palette knife	Rolling pin	Serrated scraper	Edible colourings
4" Palette knife	Pair of marzipan spacers	Nylon piping bag	Icing tubes

The above are the items of equipment used in making the cakes that appear in our book. Most of them were designed by us, and they are all obtainable through the Company's Mail Order Department.

You will find each item, and many more, featured in our catalogue, which can be obtained from:

Mary Ford Cake Artistry Centre Ltd.
28–30 Southbourne Grove, Southbourne,
Bournemouth BH6 3RA.

**Cake decorating courses are held at the Mary Ford Centre.
For further details please apply to the above address**

Mary Ford Tube No.'s showing their shapes.

| 0 | 1 | 2 | 3 | 4 | 5 | 6 | 7 | 13 | 22 | 32 | 42 | 43 | 44 | 57 | 58 | 59 |

**The above are all the icing tubes used in this book.
Please note that these are Mary Ford tubes, but comparable tubes may be used.**

1. 1st stage of 6-dot
   sequence, pipe 3 dots.

2. 2nd stage,
   pipe 2 further dots.

3. 3rd stage, pipe last
   dot to complete sequence.

4. Graduated bulbs.

5. Shell.

6. Cone-shaped shell.

7. Rosette.

8. 'C' line.

9. Bold 'C'.

10. 'S' line.

11. Rope.

12. Curved rope.

13. Spiral shell.

14. 'C' scroll.

15. 'S' scroll.

16. Left-to-right scroll.

17. Right-to-left scroll.

Various Writing Styles.

ABCDEFGHIJKLMNOPQRSTUVWXYZ ÆØ 1234567890

ABCDEFGHIJKLMNOPQRSTUVWXYZ ÆØ 1234567890

A ABCDEEFGHIJKLMNOPQRRSTTUVWXYZ

ABCDEEFGHIJKLLMNOPQRSTUVWXYZ 12345678890

ABCDEFGHIJKLMNOPQRSTUVWXYZ 1234567890

ABCDEFGHIJKLMNOPQRSTUVWXYZ 1234567890

ABCDEFGHIJKLMNOPQRSTUVWXYZ ÆØ 1234567890

ABCDEFGHIJKLMNOPQRSTUVWXYZ

ABCDEFGHIJKLMNOPQRSTUVWXYZ 1234567890

ABCDEFGHIJKLMNOPQRSTUVWXYZ 1234567890

ABCDEFGHIJKLMNOPQRSTUVWXYZ 1234567890

ABCDEFGHIJKLMNOPQRSTUVWXYZ

Making and filling a greaseproof piping bag

1. A sheet of greaseproof paper – 12″×8″ – required.

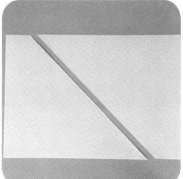

2. Cut sheet diagonally as shown.

3. Turn one triangle to position shown.

4. Fold paper from right to centre.

5. Lift corner from left to right.

6. Fold under and pull into shape.

7. Fold in loose ends and cut section. Fold back to secure.

8. Cut off tip of bag and drop in tube.

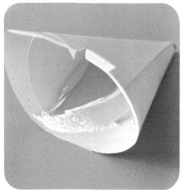

9. Using a palette knife, half fill bag with Royal Icing.

10. Carefully fold and roll the open end to seal bag, which is then ready for use.

11. To make a LEAF BAG repeat 1–7 and then flatten tip.

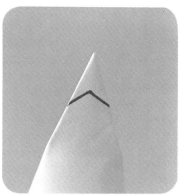

12. Picture showing shape of tip to be cut.

13. Now cut tip.

14. For using TWO COLOURS partially fill one side of bag with one colour.

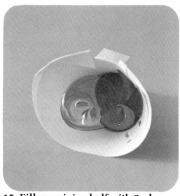

15. Fill remaining half with 2nd colour. Repeat 10.

16. Picture showing effect of using two colours of Royal Icing.

How to marzipan

17. Picture showing a matured fruit cake with lining paper removed.

18. Upturn cake, place on board (3″ larger) and if required brush on spirits and glycerine.

19. Using icing sugar for dusting, roll marzipan between spacers (approx: ⅜″ thick), as shown.

20. Cut marzipan to size using the cake tin (in which the cake was baked) as guide.

21. After removing surplus marzipan brush off any loose icing sugar.

22. Jam the marzipan with boiling apricot puree by applying it with a palette knife.

23. Lay cake onto the jammed marzipan.

24. Upturn cake and replace on board.

25. Picture showing a square cake (which is prepared in the same way as a round cake).

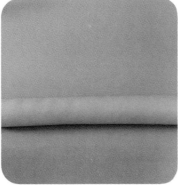

26. Form remaining marzipan into a sausage shape.

27. Now roll the marzipan into a thin strip (wide enough to cover the cake side).

28. Cut marzipan for side (length=approx: 3 times diameter) and then jam as in 22.

29. Fix marzipan to cake side and trim off surplus (L.D. approx: 3 days).

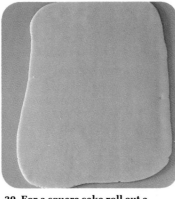

30. For a square cake roll out a sheet of marzipan to cover the 4 sides.

31. Cut the sheet into 4 separate strips to fit sides.

32. Jam and fix each strip then trim (L.D. approx: 3 days).

HOW TO CUT A WEDGE
33. After marzipanning, cut wedge from cake, as shown.

34. Replace wedge.

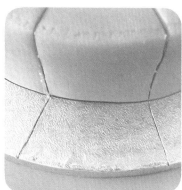

35. Mark board to show position of wedge. Place cake on turntable.

HOW TO COAT A CAKE
36. Spread Royal Icing around side of cake with a palette knife.

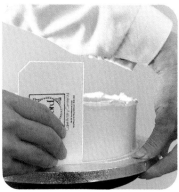

37. Place hands in position shown (holding the scraper against the cake side).

38. Holding scraper steady with one hand, revolve the turntable one complete turn with the other hand.

39. Repeat 36–38 until side is smooth.

40. Using the palette knife, remove surplus icing fom cake.

41. Immediately remove wedge.

42. Clean sides of wedge and replace (L.D. 12 hrs).

43. Using the palette knife, place Royal Icing on top of the cake.

44. Using the palette knife in a paddling movement, spread the icing evenly over the cake top.

45. Using a stainless steel rule, start to level the icing.

46. Continue to use the rule in a backwards and forwards motion to level icing.

47. Picture showing coated cake.

48. Remove surplus icing from edges of cake top and wedge (L.D. 12 hrs). Repeat 36–48 twice more.

11

49. 1½ yards of satin ribbon on a piece of greaseproof paper – approx: 8″×6″ required.

50. Fold the paper over the centre of the ribbon.

51. Fold the paper and ribbon in half and place to wedge.

52. Replace wedge.

53. Roll up equal lengths of ribbon ends and fix to side of cake.

HOW TO COAT A BOARD.
54. Picture showing hands and scraper in readiness to coat board.

55. Holding scraper steady in one hand, revolve the turntable one complete turn with the other (see picture 38).

56. For coating a square (or hexagonal, etc.) cake, coat the opposite sides (L.D. 12 hrs).

57. Now coat remaining sides (L.D. 12 hrs).

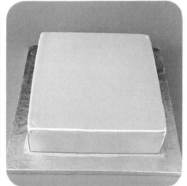

58. Coat the top as for round cake (L.D. 12 hrs). Repeat 56–58 twice more.

HOW TO MAKE A SUGAR PASTE ROSE BUD.
59. Roll a piece of sugar paste into the shape shown.

60. Flatten back to form sharp edge.

61. Roll up the sugar paste as shown.

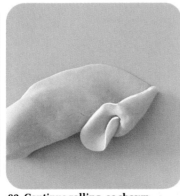

62. Continue rolling, as shown.

63. Fold over remaining sugar paste.

64. Remove surplus sugar paste, then bend back edge to form bud.

12

HOW TO MAKE A SUGAR PASTE ROSE.
65. Repeat 59–64 but finishing with bud in upright position.

66. Roll out sugar paste and flatten one end.

67. Cut away surplus leaving the petal.

68. Wrap petal around the bud and slightly dampen with water to fix.

69. Repeat 66–68 for the second petal.

70. Repeat 66–68 making and fixing larger petals until size of rose required is obtained.

MAKING ROYAL ICING BIRDS.
71. Pipe wings on waxed paper, working from left to right (No.1) (L.D. 12 hrs).

72. Pipe tail on waxed paper (two types shown) (No.1).

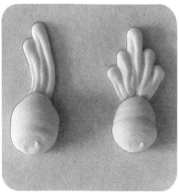

73. Pipe body against tail (No.1).

74. Lifting icing bag pipe neck, head and beak (No.1).

75. Immediately fix wings to body (L.D. 12 hrs).

MAKING SUGAR BELLS
76. Pipe a bulb on waxed paper (No.3).

77. Pipe a second bulb on top (No.3).

78. Sprinkle granulated sugar over the bulbs (then leave until outside of bulbs are dry).

79. Scoop out unset Royal Icing from centre of bell.

80. Pipe-in hammer (No.1).

13

PIPING SUGAR FLOWERS & ROSES

PIPING SUGAR FLOWERS
81. Picture showing items required=flower nail, waxed paper and piping bag with petal tube (No.58).

82. Fix a square of waxed paper to top of flower nail and hold in position shown.

83. Keeping thick end of tube to the centre of flower, pipe 1st petal.

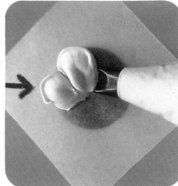

84. Turn nail and pipe next petal.

85. Turn nail and pipe 3rd petal.

86. Turn nail and pipe 4th petal.

87. Turn nail and pipe 5th petal.

88. Turn nail and pipe the last petal.

89. Picture showing the piped petals.

90. Pipe a centre bulb (No.2) (L.D. 24 hrs).

PIPING SUGAR ROSES
91. Form a cone of marzipan.

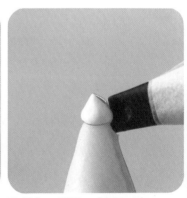

92. Using stiff Royal Icing, pipe the centre of the rose (No.57).

93. Pipe a petal behind the centre (No.57).

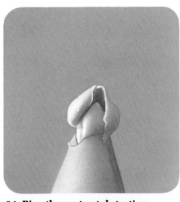

94. Pipe the next petal starting inside the 1st petal (No.57).

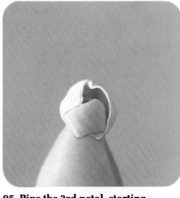

95. Pipe the 3rd petal, starting inside the 2nd petal and ending over part of the 1st petal (No.57) (L.D. 15 m).

96. Repeat 93–95 for 5 petals around outside of rose (L.D. 24 hrs). Remove from cone.

14

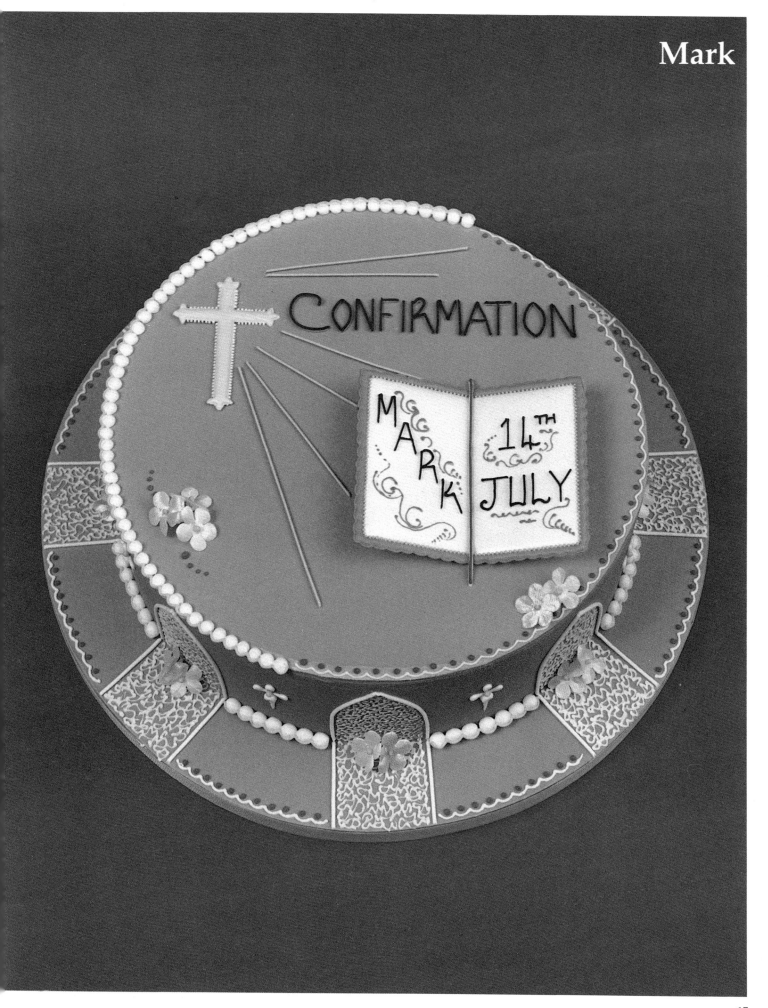

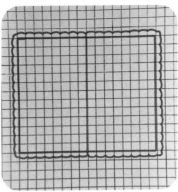

1. Drawing showing template of Confirmation Card.

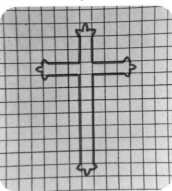

2. Drawing showing template of a Cross.

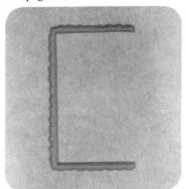

3. Outline and flood-in on waxed paper the part of the Confirmation Card shown (L.D. 4 hrs).

4. Outline and flood-in on another piece of waxed paper the part of the Confirmation Card shown (L.D. 4 hrs).

5. Outline and flood-in on waxed paper the Cross (L.D. 12 hrs).

6. Outline and flood-in the left-hand page of Confirmation Card (L.D. 24 hrs).

7. Outline and flood-in the right-hand page of the Confirmation Card (L.D. 24 hrs).

8. Pipe dots around the Cross (No.1) (L.D. 12 hrs).

9. Pipe name of choice on Confirmation Card (No.1) then overpipe name (No.1).

10. Pipe appropriate date on Confirmation Card (No.1) then overpipe date (No.1).

11. Pipe curved lines and dots each side of name (No.0).

12. Pipe curved lines and dots around date (No.0).

13. Pipe dots inside each Confirmation Card edge, as shown (No.1).

14. Fix Cross to cake-top, as shown.

15. Fix Confirmation Card to cake-top in open position, as shown.

16. Pipe a line along the centre of the Confirmation Card (No.2) then overpipe the No.2 line (No.1).

NOTE: Before attempting to decorate this cake, please study the whole sequence of photographs and notes and ensure you have the proper equipment and materials, as well as sufficient time. Additional information can be found on pages 4-14 and 96.

17. Pipe 'CONFIRMATION' on cake-top (No.1) then overpipe 'CONFIRMATION' (No.1).

18. Pipe lines from Cross (No.1) then overpipe lines (No.1).

19. Pipe 8 equal distance windows around cake-side (No.2) (T).

20. Filigree each window (No.1).

21. Pipe continuation window lines across the cake-board (No.2).

22. Filigree between each pair of cake-board No.2 lines (No.1).

23. Pipe bulbs around the part of the cake-top edge shown (No.2).

24. Pipe a line over each cake-top bulb (No.1).

25. Pipe a scalloped line around the remaining part of the cake-top edge (No.1).

26. Pipe a dot in each scallop (No.1).

27. Pipe bulbs between each window around cake-base (No.2).

28. Pipe a line over each cake-base bulb (No.1).

29. Pipe pear-shape bulbs between each cake-side window (No.1).

30. Pipe a further pear-shape bulb and a dot, as shown (No.1).

31. Pipe scalloped lines and dots between cake-board windows, as shown (No.1).

32. Fix artificial flowers of choice and pipe graduated dots, as required (No.1).

17

Memory

NOTE: *Before attempting to decorate this cake, please study the whole sequence of photographs and notes and ensure you have the proper equipment and materials, as well as sufficient time. Additional information can be found on pages 4-14 and 96.*

1. Picture showing an oval cake on a 12″ round gold board.

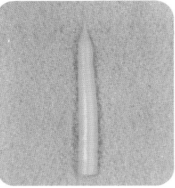

2. Pipe a 2″ line on to coloured granulated sugar (¼″ diameter tube) to form lily flower spadix.

3. Immediately cover spadix in the coloured granulated sugar (L.D. 12 hrs) (7 required).

4. Roll out and cut a sugar paste lily petal, as shown.

5. Fix spadix to centre of lily petal, as shown.

6. Fold petal over spadix, as shown.

7. Fold and fix petal, as shown.

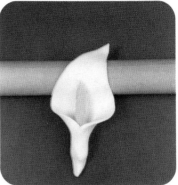

8. Place lily in the position shown (L.D. 12 hrs) (7 required).

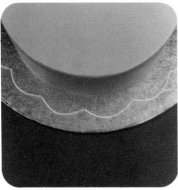

9. Pipe 16 curved lines equal distance from cake, as shown.

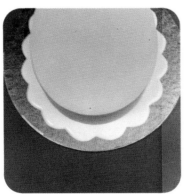

10. Flood-in between cake-base and the No.2 lines (L.D. 12 hrs).

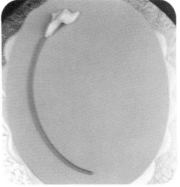

11. Fix lily to cake-top, as shown, then pipe a curved line to form stem (No.4).

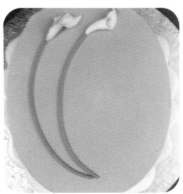

12. Fix a second lily, as shown, then pipe a stem (No.4).

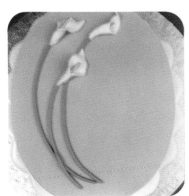

13. Fix a third lily, as shown, then pipe a stem (No.4).

14. Pipe leaves, as shown (Leaf bag).

15. Pipe a stem to each leaf (No.4).

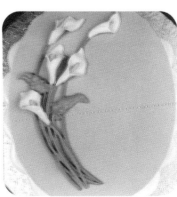

16. Fix two further lilies, as shown, then pipe a stem to each lily (No.4).

19

NOTE: *Before attempting to decorate this cake, please study the whole sequence of photographs and notes and ensure you have the proper equipment and materials, as well as sufficient time. Additional information can be found on pages 4-14 and 96.*

17. Fix a ribbon bow to spray of lilies.

18. Pipe message of choice to cake-top (No.1) then overpipe message (No.1).

19. Pipe a 'C' scroll to cake-top edge, as shown (No.43).

20. Pipe a further 'C' scroll to cake-top edge, as shown (No.43).

21. Pipe further 'C' scrolls around cake-top edge, as shown (No.43).

22. Pipe shells around the remaining part of the cake-top edge, as shown (No.2).

23. Overpipe each scroll (No.3).

24. Overpipe each scroll (No.2).

25. Overpipe each scroll (No.1).

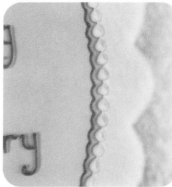

26. Pipe a curved line inside each cake-top shell (No.1).

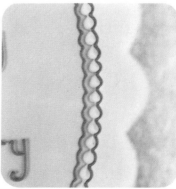

27. Pipe a line over each cake-top shell (No.1).

28. Pipe shells around cake-base (beneath cake-top scrolls) (No.43).

29. Pipe shells around remaining part of cake-base (No.3).

30. Pipe a line over each No.43 cake-base shell (No.2) then over-pipe each No.2 line (No.1).

31. Pipe a line over each No.3 cake-base shell (No.1).

32. Fix two lilies to cake-board and then pipe stems (No.4).

1. Drawing showing template of plaques.

2. Outline and flood-in an oval plaque on waxed paper (L.D. 24 hrs).

3. Outline and flood-in 4 curved plaques on waxed paper (L.D. 24 hrs).

4. Pipe-in on waxed paper the parts of the figures shown (L.D. 20 m).

5. Pipe-in further parts of the figures, as shown (L.D. 20 m).

6. Pipe-in further parts of the figures, as shown (L.D. 20 m).

7. Pipe-in further parts of the figures, as shown (L.D. 20 m).

8. Pipe-in further parts of the figures, as shown (L.D. 20 m).

9. Pipe-in further parts of the figures, as shown (L.D. 20 m).

10. Pipe-in final parts of the figures (L.D. 20 m).

11. Paint figures with edible colouring (L.D. 24 hrs).

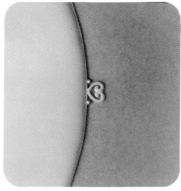

12. Pipe a heart-shape design on edge of oval plaque and add a dot each side (No.1).

13. Repeat 12 around plaque and then fix figures to plaque (L.D. 12 hrs).

14. Pipe ½" high heart shape on waxed paper (No.1). Overpipe (No.1) and then pipe a dot (No.1) (L.D. 12 hrs) (8 required).

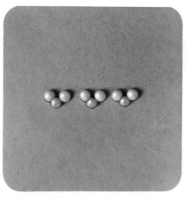

15. Picture showing sequence of dot edging.

16. Pipe dot edging around the 4 curved plaques and then pipe message of choice (No.1) (L.D. 12 hrs).

17. Fix all plaques to cake top in positions shown.

18. Pipe shells around top edge of cake (No.44).

19. Pipe shells around base of cake (No.43).

20. Pipe short vertical lines on cake sides in positions shown (No.2).

21. Pipe curved lines on cake board, as shown (No.2).

22. Fix artificial flowers in the positions shown at the base of the cake.

23. Pipe a suspended line from each short line to board line, as shown (No.2).

24. Pipe a suspended line each side of the suspended line (No.2).

25. Pipe a suspended line each side of the suspended lines (No.2).

26. Repeat 25.

27. Repeat 26.

28. Pipe a bulb at each top join of the suspended lines and pipe shells against the board lines (No.2).

29. Pipe a parallel curved line on cake board (No.2).

30. Pipe a line beside the board No.2 line (No.1) and then overpipe each bulb with a line (No.1).

31. Pipe suspended tassels and a dot on each bulb (No.2) and then pipe a line beside the board No.1 line (No.1).

32. Fix artificial flowers, horseshoes, hearts and ribbon, as shown.

23

Harvey

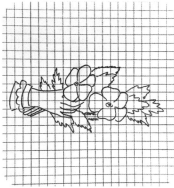

1. Drawing showing template of hand holding flowers.

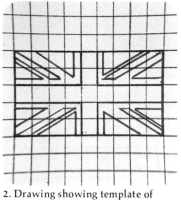

2. Drawing showing template of Union Flag.

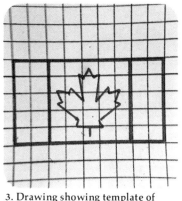

3. Drawing showing template of Canadian Flag.

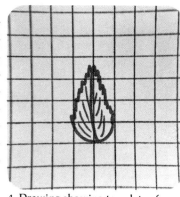

4. Drawing showing template of leaf.

5. Pipe-in on waxed paper the parts of the leaves and stems shown (No.1).

6. Pipe-in the further leaves shown (No.1).

7. Pipe-in the further leaves shown (No.1).

8. Pipe hand and sleeve (No.2).

9. Pipe flowers (No.2).

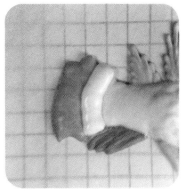

10. Pipe cuff (No.1).

11. Pipe dots along cuff edge and in each flower (No.1) then brush in lines, as shown (L.D. 24 hrs).

12. Pipe the lines shown on waxed paper (No.1).

13. Flood-in the parts shown.

14. Outline and flood-in the further parts shown (L.D. 2 hrs).

15. Flood-in the remaining parts shown (L.D. 24 hrs).

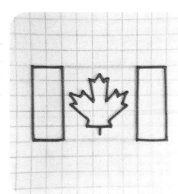

16. Pipe the lines shown on waxed paper.

25

NOTE: *Before attempting to decorate this cake, please study the whole sequence of photographs and notes and ensure you have the proper equipment and materials, as well as sufficient time. Additional information can be found on pages 4-14 and 96.*

17. Pipe the two lines shown and then flood-in the area shown (L.D. 2 hrs).

18. Flood-in the further parts shown.

19. Pipe part of the leaf shown on waxed paper (No.1).

20. Pipe remaining part of leaf (No.1).

21. Repeat 19-20 in three shades of green (24 of each shade required) (L.D. 24 hrs in position shown).

22. Fix floral runout to cake-top.

23. Fix flags to cake-top.

24. Pipe flag staffs (No.1).

25. Pipe 'Welcome' as shown (No.1) then overpipe (No.1).

26. Pipe 'Home' as shown (No.1) then overpipe (No.1).

27. Fix leaves around cake-top edge, as shown.

28. Fix leaves around cake-base, as shown.

29. Pipe a floral design to each leaf (No.2).

30. Brush lines, as shown, on each floral design.

31. Pipe a dot on the centre of each floral design (No.1).

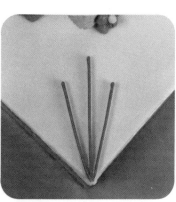

32. Pipe lines, as shown, at each cake-board corner (No.1) then overpipe (No.1).

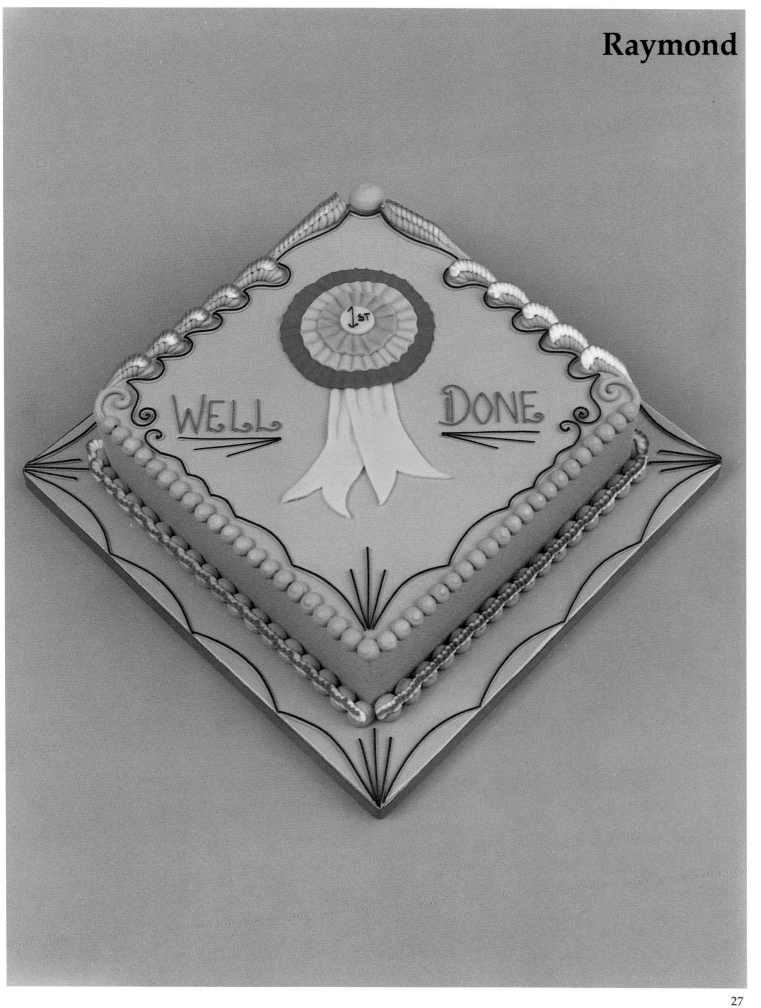

NOTE: Before attempting to decorate this cake, please study the whole sequence of photographs and notes and ensure you have the proper equipment and materials, as well as sufficient time. Additional information can be found on pages 4-14 and 96.

1. Roll out and cut a 3¼" disc of sugar paste.

2. Crimp edge of disc using the back of a knife handle.

3. Place disc on cake-top, as shown.

4. Roll out and cut a 2¼" disc of sugar paste and crimp edge.

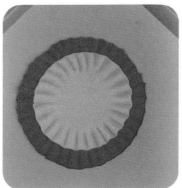

5. Place disc on first disc.

6. Roll out and cut a 1½" disc of sugar paste and crimp edge.

7. Place disc on second disc.

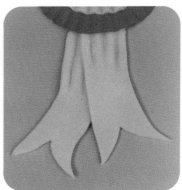

8. Roll out, cut and fix a pair of rosette ribbons.

9. Roll out, cut and fix a ¾" disc of sugar paste to rosette centre.

10. Picture showing completed rosette so far.

11. Pipe '1st' on rosette centre (No.1).

12. Pipe the word 'WELL' on cake-top (No.2) then overpipe 'WELL' (No.1).

13. Pipe the word 'DONE' on cake-top (No.2) then overpipe 'DONE' (No.1).

14. Pipe lines under 'WELL' (No.1) then overpipe the No.1 lines (No.1).

15. Pipe lines under 'DONE' (No.1) then overpipe the No.1 lines (No.1).

16. Pipe a bulb on the back cake-top corner (No.4).

28

NOTE: Before attempting to decorate this cake, please study the whole sequence of photographs and notes and ensure you have the proper equipment and materials, as well as sufficient time. Additional information can be found on pages 4–14 and 96.

17. Pipe a right-to-left 'S' scroll from bulb, as shown (No.4).

18. Pipe a left-to-right 'S' scroll from bulb, as shown (No.4).

19. Pipe a 'C' scroll at the end of each 'S' scroll (No.4).

20. Pipe further 'C' scrolls along the cake-top edges shown (No.4).

21. Pipe a 'C' line at the end of each row of 'C' scrolls (No.4).

22. Pipe bulbs along each of the remaining cake-top edges (No.3).

23. Pipe curved lines beside the scrolls along the cake-top edge shown (No.2).

24. Pipe curved lines beside the scrolls along the cake-top edge shown (No.2).

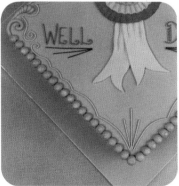

25. Pipe curved lines beside the shells along the cake-top edge shown and the straight lines shown (No.2).

26. Pipe curved lines beside the shells along the cake-top edge shown (No.2).

27. Pipe bulbs around cake-base (No.3).

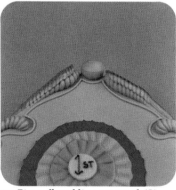

28. Pipe a fluted line over each 'S' scroll (using two colours in bag) (No.57).

29. Pipe a fluted line over each 'C' scroll (using two colours in bag) (No.57).

30. Pipe a fluted line over each cake-base bulb (using two colours in bag) (No.57).

31. Pipe curved and straight lines around cake-board, as shown (No.2).

32. Overpipe each No.2 line (No.1).

Pedro

NOTE: *Before attempting to decorate this cake, please study the whole sequence of photographs and notes and ensure you have the proper equipment and materials, as well as sufficient time. Additional information can be found on pages 4-14 and 96.*

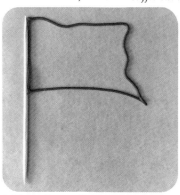

1. Pipe a flag outline on waxed paper to a cocktail stick (No.2).

2. Flood-in the flag (L.D. 24 hrs).

3. Pipe message of choice on flag (No.1) (L.D. 2 hrs).

4. Make a cone of waxed paper.

5. Pipe four 2″ lines down cone, as shown (No.2).

6. Pipe further lines, as shown (No.2).

7. Pipe further lines, as shown (No.2).

8. Pipe a bulb at top of cone (No.2) to complete a tassel (4 required) (L.D. 12 hrs).

9. A cake baked in a 2pt. pudding basin and upturned on a 16″ round board required.

10. Marzipan and coat the cake in the normal way.

11. Coat the board with Royal Icing.

12. Pipe a line along the edge of the board (No.32) (L.D. 2 hrs).

13. Overpipe the No.32 line in the manner shown (No.32) (L.D. 2 hrs).

14. Overpipe the No.32 line in the manner shown (No.32) (L.D. 2 hrs).

15. Pipe short lines around the crown of the sombrero, as shown (No.22).

16. Pipe a line across each of the No.22 lines (No.22).

31

17. Pipe the further lines shown (No.22).

18. Pipe the further lines shown in colour (No.22).

19. Pipe the further lines shown (No.22).

20. Pipe the further lines shown (No.22).

21. Repeat 7–10 once and then 7–12 once.

22. Continue piping 7–10 in one colour (No.22).

23. Pipe crossed lines in colour, as shown (No.22).

24. Continue piping rows in the manner shown (No.22).

25. Continue piping rows in the manner shown (No.22).

26. Continue piping crossed lines over the sombrero brim (No.22).

27. Pipe lines on the sombrero crown, as shown (No.22).

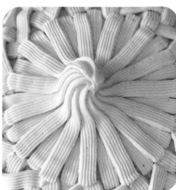

28. Pipe further lines on the crown, as shown (No.22).

29. Pipe bulbs around the sombrero rim, as shown (No.2).

30. Pipe suspended lines from each bulb and finish tassel with a top bulb (No.2).

31. Fix the 4 cone tassels to the cake base with a piped rope (No.2).

32. Fix the flag to the crown of Pedro's sombrero.

1. Serrated scraper required.

2. On final coating use serrated scraper to form pattern around cake.

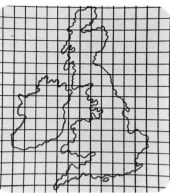

3. Drawing showing template of the British Isles.

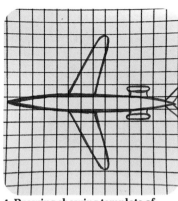

4. Drawing showing template of an aeroplane.

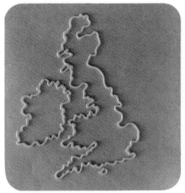

5. Outline the British Isles on waxed paper (No.2).

6. Flood-in the British Isles (L.D. 24 hrs).

7. Outline and flood-in on waxed paper the parts of the aeroplane shown (L.D. 1 hr).

8. Flood-in remaining parts of the aeroplane and a separate tail, as shown (L.D. 24 hrs).

9. Pipe shells around edge of cake top (No.4).

10. Pipe shells around base of cake (No.4) (L.D. 2 hrs).

11. Overpipe each top shell with a curved line (No.3).

12. Overpipe each base shell with a curved line (No.3).

13. Overpipe each No.3 top line (No.2).

14. Overpipe each No.3 base line (No.2).

15. Pipe curved lines on the cake top, as shown (No.2).

16. Pipe further curved lines on the cake top, as shown (No.2).

34

17. Pipe short curved lines on cake top, as shown (No.1).

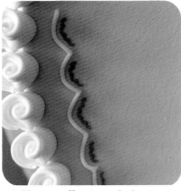

18. Pipe a scallop in each short curved line on the cake top (No.1).

19. Decorate the British Isles with edible colouring, as shown.

20. Fix tail to aeroplane.

21. Decorate aeroplane with piped lines and dots, as shown (No.1).

22. Fix British Isles and aeroplane to cake top.

23. Pipe message of choice (No.1).

24. Complete message of choice (No.2)

25. Pipe lines beside message (No's 1 & 2).

26. Pipe seagulls around message (No.1).

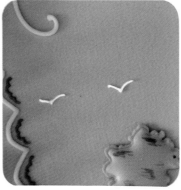

27. Pipe seagulls around British Isles (No.1).

28. Overpipe the top shell curved lines (No.1).

29. Overpipe the base shell curved lines (No.1).

30. Pipe curved lines around the cake board, as shown (No.2).

31. Pipe scallops and dots on board, as shown (No.1).

32. Fix artificial flowers to cake base and ribbon to board edge.

Merrie

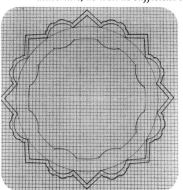

1. Drawing showing template of cake-top runout.

2. Outline and flood-in on waxed paper the cake-top runout (L.D. 24 hrs).

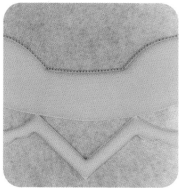

3. Pipe single dots around inside of runout (No.1).

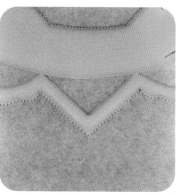

4. Pipe single dots around outside of runout (No.1).

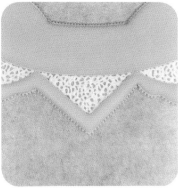

5. Filigree each runout aperture (No.0).

6. Picture showing stage 1 of fir spray. Pipe curved line, as shown (No.1).

7. Stage 2. Pipe spikes from curved line (No.1).

8. Stage 3. Pipe clusters of dots to form fir cones (No.2).

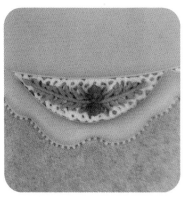

9. Pipe fir spray on each of the runout semi-circles (L.D. 12 hrs).

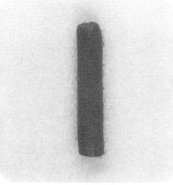

10. Pipe a line on to granulated sugar (1/4″ diameter tube) to form candle.

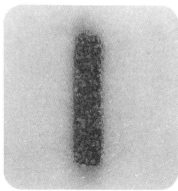

11. Immediately cover candle with granulated sugar (L.D. 24 hrs) (one each @ 2¼″, 2″ and 1½″ required).

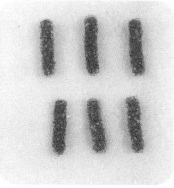

12. Make 8 further candles (No.4) each ¾″ long (L.D. 24 hrs).

13. Pipe holly leaves on waxed paper (No.1) and immediately fix over 1″ dowling (L.D. 24 hrs).

14. Pipe a line around cake-top edge (No.3) (L.D. 1 hr).

15. Overpipe the No.3 line (No.2) and immediately fix runout to cake-top.

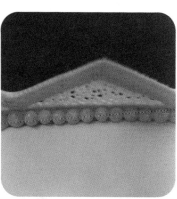

16. Pipe bulbs around cake-top edge (under runout) (No.2) (T).

NOTE: *Before attempting to decorate this cake, please study the whole sequence of photographs and notes and ensure you have the proper equipment and materials, as well as sufficient time. Additional information can be found on pages 4-14 and 96.*

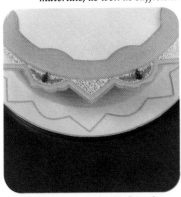

17. Pipe lines around cake-board, as indicated (No.2).

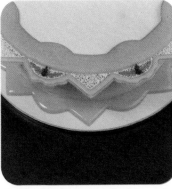

18. Flood-in between cake-base and the No.2 cake-board lines (L.D. 12 hrs).

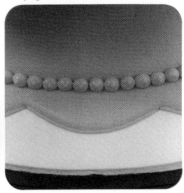

19. Pipe bulbs around cake-base (No.2).

20. Pipe single dots around cake-base runout (No.1).

21. Pipe fir sprays on cake-board in positions indicated.

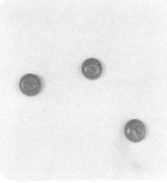

22. Pipe bulbs on cake-top, as shown (No.2).

23. Immediately fix the ¼″ diameter candles to cake-top bulbs, as shown (L.D. 1 hr).

24. Fix curved holly leaves to the base of each candle, as shown.

25. Fix further curved holly leaves, as shown.

26. Pipe holly berries around each candle base (No.1).

27. Pipe a flame to each candle (No.4 – 2 colours in bag) then pipe shells to represent dripping wax (No.2).

28. Pipe message of choice to cake-top (No.1) then overpipe message (No.1).

29. Fix remaining candles to cake-top runout, as shown.

30. Pipe a flame to each cake-top runout candle (No.2 – 2 colours in bag) then fix holly leaves, as shown.

31. Fix 8 holly leaves around cake-base in positions indicated.

32. Pipe a berry at each cake-base holly leaf.

NOTE: Before attempting to decorate this cake, please study the whole sequence of photographs and notes and ensure you have the proper equipment and materials, as well as sufficient time. Additional information can be found on pages 4-14 and 96.

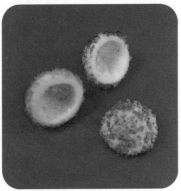

1. Ten piped sugar bells required.

2. Pipe two lines across cake, as shown (No.4).

3. Continue piping lines down cake-sides (No.4) (T).

4. Continue piping lines across cake-board (No.4).

5. Fix two bells to cake-top centre and pipe a clapper to each bell (No.1).

6. Pipe a curved line, as shown (No.2).

7. Pipe a further curved line, as shown (No.2).

8. Pipe a further curved line, as shown (No.2).

9. Repeat 6-8 in opposite directions on other side of bells.

10. Pipe stems and leaves on all No.2 lines, as indicated (No.1).

11. Pipe berries to each spray (No.1).

12. Pipe a curved line between cake-board No.2 lines (No.2).

13. Pipe stems, leaves and berries on each cake-board curved line (No.1).

14. Pipe a line outside each No.4 line (No.3) then overpipe each No.4 line (No.3) (T as necessary).

15. Pipe a line outside each No.3 line (No.2) then overpipe each No.3 line (No.2) (T as necessary).

16. Pipe a line outside each No.2 line (No.1) then overpipe each No.2 line (No.1) (T as necessary).

17. Overpipe each inner No.1 line (No.1) (T as necessary).

18. Pipe leaves outside each No.1 line, as shown (No.1) (T as necessary).

19. Pipe a berry to each outside leaf (No.1).

20. Pipe first part of message (No.1) then overpipe message (No.1).

21. Pipe second part of message (No.1) then overpipe message (No.1).

22. Pipe a line around cake-base but excluding centre panels (No.43) (L.D. 1 hr).

23. Pipe 'S' scrolls at the front centre of the cake-top edge (No.42). Repeat at back cake-top edge.

24. Pipe a 'C' scroll at each of the cake-top front and back corners, as shown (No.42).

25. Pipe a 'C' scroll and a 'C' line at each cake-top corner (No.42).

26. Pipe an 'S' and a 'C' scroll at each cake-top corner (No.42).

27. Repeat 23–26 at the cake-base.

28. Overpipe each scroll and 'C' line (No.2).

29. Overpipe each scroll and 'C' line (No.1).

30. Pipe a rope around cake-board edge but excluding centre panels (No.42).

31. Pipe 3 lines, as shown, at each cake-board corner (No.2) then overpipe each line (No.1).

32. Pipe 4 graduated dots between each cake-top 'S' scroll (No.2) then fix bells and decorations of choice.

41

Bobbie

NOTE: Before attempting to decorate this cake, please study the whole sequence of photographs and notes and ensure you have the proper equipment and materials, as well as sufficient time. Additional information can be found on pages 4-14 and 96.

1. Picture showing cake scraper required.

2. Use cake scraper when coating side of cake.

3. Pipe the lines shown on cake-top (No.4).

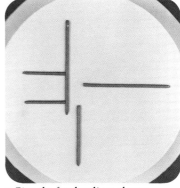

4. Pipe the further lines shown (No.4).

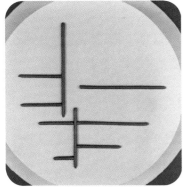

5. Pipe the further lines shown (No.4).

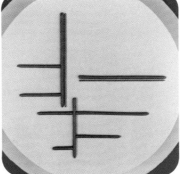

6. Pipe the further lines shown (No.2).

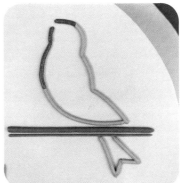

7. Pipe outline of a robin (No.3).

8. Decorate robin, as shown (No.1).

9. Pipe 'CHRISTMAS' where shown (No.1) then overpipe 'CHRISTMAS' (No.1).

10. Pipe a wavy line, as shown (No.2).

11. Pipe dots, as shown (No.1).

12. Pipe outline of holly leaves (No.1).

13. Pipe outline of holly leaves (No.1).

14. Pipe bulbs of various sizes (No.2).

15. Pipe snowflakes, as shown (No.1).

16. Pipe bulbs around cake-top side (No.3) (T).

17. Pipe bulbs around cake-side, as shown (No.3) (T).

18. Pipe shells around cake-side, as shown (No.2) (T).

19. Pipe shells around cake-side, as shown (No.2) (T).

20. Pipe bulbs around cake-base (No.3).

21. Pipe a line on each cake-side top shell, as shown (No.2).

22. Pipe spikes around cake-side, as shown (No.2).

23. Pipe a line over each cake-side bulb, as shown (No.2).

24. Pipe a line against each cake-side No.2 line (No.1).

25. Pipe spikes around cake-side, as shown (No.1).

26. Pipe a line over each cake-base shell (No.2).

27. Overpipe each cake-base No.2 line (No.1).

28. Pipe spikes around cake-base, as shown (No.1).

29. Pipe bulbs around the centre of the cake-board (No.2).

30. Pipe a line over each cake-board bulb (No.2).

31. Overpipe each cake-board No.2 line (No.1).

32. Pipe spikes around cake-board, as shown (No.1).

44

NOTE: *Before attempting to decorate this cake, please study the whole sequence of photographs and notes and ensure you have the proper equipment and materials, as well as sufficient time. Additional information can be found on pages 4-14 and 96.*

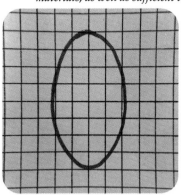

1. Drawing showing template of plaque.

2. Outline and flood-in on waxed paper four plaques (L.D. 24 hrs).

3. Four lovebirds required.

4. Fold a paper disc three times and mark the curve shown.

5. Cut along the marked curve, unfold and place on cake-top under a suitable weight.

6. Pipe curved lines around the disc (No.3) then remove disc.

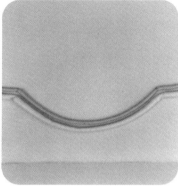

7. Pipe a line inside each No.3 line (No.2).

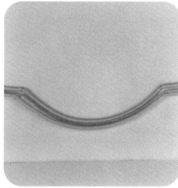

8. Overpipe each No.3 line (No.2).

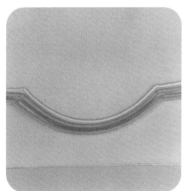

9. Pipe a line inside each No.2 line (No.1).

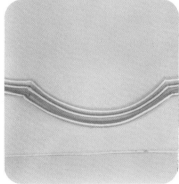

10. Overpipe each No.2 line (No.1).

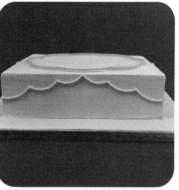

11. Pipe curved lines on each cake-side (No.3) (T).

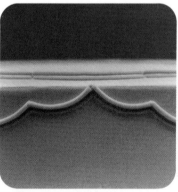

12. Pipe a line beneath each cake-side No.3 line (No.2) (T).

13. Overpipe each cake-side No.3 line (No.2) (T).

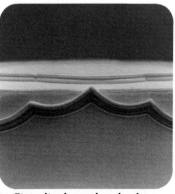

14. Pipe a line beneath each cake-side No.2 line (No.1) (T).

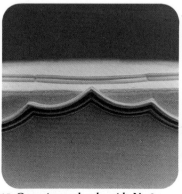

15. Overpipe each cake-side No.2 line (No.1) (T).

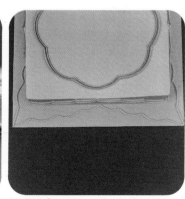

16. Pipe lines around cake-board, as indicated (No.3).

17. Pipe a line inside each cake-board No.3 line (No.2).

18. Overpipe each cake-board No.3 line (No.2).

19. Pipe a line inside each cake-board No.2 line (No.1).

20. Overpipe each cake-board No.2 line (No.1).

21. Pipe a row of dots around the edge of each plaque (No.1).

22. Pipe initials of choice on each plaque (No.1) then overpipe initials (No.1).

23. Paint initials with edible food colouring.

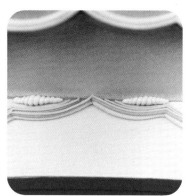

24. Pipe barrel scrolls around cake-base in positions indicated (No.2).

25. Pipe further barrel scrolls around each cake-base corner, as shown (No.2).

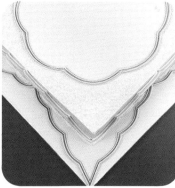

26. Filigree around cake-top edge, as shown (No.1).

27. Filigree around each cake-side, as shown (No.1) (T).

28. Filigree around cake-board, as shown (No. 1).

29. Fix a plaque to each cake-side, as shown.

30. Fix a lovebird to the centre of each cake-top edge.

31. Fix feathers and leaves to each cake-base corner.

32. Fix artificial rose to each cake-base corner.

Sandra

NOTE: Before attempting to decorate this cake, please study the whole sequence of photographs and notes and ensure you have the proper equipment and materials, as well as sufficient time. Additional information can be found on pages 4-14 and 96.

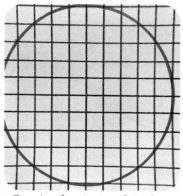

1. Drawing showing template of a 2″ diameter circle.

2. Pipe a 2″ diameter circle on waxed paper (No.3) (L.D. 10 m) (2 required).

3. Overpipe each circle but with a slightly reduced diameter as shown (No.3) (L.D. 10 m).

4. Continue overpiping 3 more times – with 10 m interval between each – to give a conical effect (No.3) (L.D. 1 hr).

5. Continue overpiping 3 more times – with 10 m interval between each – to form cones (No.3) (L.D. 12 hrs).

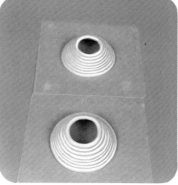

6. Picture showing completed cones.

7. Fix cones together to form bird ornament (L.D. 12 hrs).

8. Drawing showing template of a large and small heart shape.

9. Pipe a large heart shape on waxed paper (No.2) (32 required) and then a small heart shape (No.1) (16 required) (L.D. 1 hr).

10. Pipe a floral pattern inside each large heart shape, as shown (No.1) (L.D. 12 hrs).

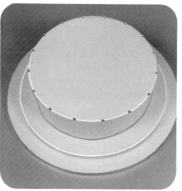

11. Prepare cake and boards, as shown, then mark cake-top edge into 16 portions with piped dots.

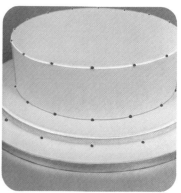

12. Mark base of cake and small board with parallel dots, as shown.

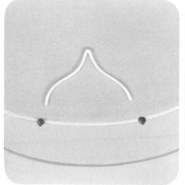

13. Pipe curved line pattern on cake top, as shown (No.2).

14. Continue piping pattern around cake top.

15. Remove the top edge marker dots and pipe a line around the top edge of cake (No.2).

16. Repeat 13–14 on cake board but in reverse, as shown.

NOTE: Before attempting to decorate this cake, please study the whole sequence of photographs and notes and ensure you have the proper equipment and materials, as well as sufficient time. Additional information can be found on pages 4-14 and 96.

17. Flood-in cake-top and board pattern. (L.D. 12 hrs).

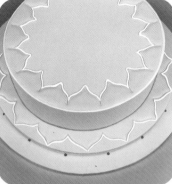

18. Pipe a line beside each pattern line (No.2).

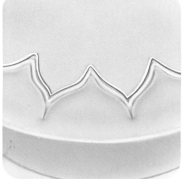

19. Pipe a line beside each No.2 line (No.1) and then overpipe each No.2 line (No.1).

20. Pipe 'S' scrolls in the position shown and then repeat around top edge of cake (No.2).

21. Pipe shells around base of cake (No.2).

22. Fix large hearts to top edge and board, as shown. (Support until dry).

23. Fix ribbon to small board edge. Pipe curved line on large board and then around board edge (No.2).

24. Remove marker dots and flood-in outer edge of large board, as shown.

25. Pipe shells around edge of small board (No.2).

26. Overpipe board runout with curved lines and floral designs, as shown (No.1).

27. Pipe plain shells around top edge of bird ornament (No.1).

28. Pipe small suspended loops and dots around top edge of ornament (No.1) and fix sugar rose in centre.

29. Fix small hearts around base of ornament.

30. Pipe a line linking the small hearts (No.1) (L.D. 12 hrs).

31. Fix sugar birds to edge of ornament and then fix ornament to top centre of cake.

32. Pipe shells around edge of the large board (No.1) and fix ribbon around edge.

50

NOTE: *Before attempting to decorate this cake, please study the whole sequence of photographs and notes and ensure you have the proper equipment and materials, as well as sufficient time. Additional information can be found on pages 4–14 and 96.*

1. Pipe a 'C' scroll from centre of one side to corner, as shown (No.44).

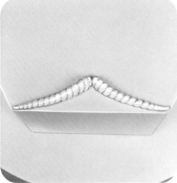

2. Pipe the opposite scroll (No.44).

3. Repeat 1 and 2 on cake top, as shown.

4. Pipe an 'S' scroll from centre top edge to corner (No.44).

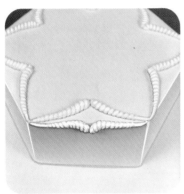

5. Pipe the opposite scroll (No.44) then repeat around each top edge.

6. Pipe spiral shells linked by a curved rope along each base (No.44).

7. Pipe bulbs inside the curved rope along cake base (No.3).

8. Overpipe the left 'C' scroll (No.3).

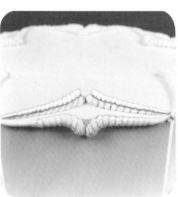

9. Overpipe the right 'C' scroll (No.3) and then repeat 8–9 on all 'C' scrolls.

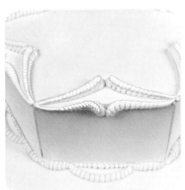

10. Overpipe the left 'S' scroll (No.3).

11. Overpipe the right 'S' scroll (No.3) and then repeat 10–11 on all 'S' scrolls.

12. Overpipe each curved rope (No.3).

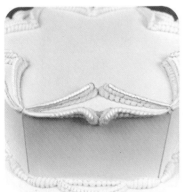

13. Overpipe each 'C' scroll (No.2).

14. Overpipe each 'S' scroll (No.2).

15. Overpipe each curved rope (No.2).

16. Pipe curved lines on cake side, as shown (No.2) (T).

17. Pipe a line under the No.2 line on cake side (No.1) (T).

18. Pipe a line against the No.2 line on cake side (No.1) (T).

19. Pipe suspended lines across the scrolls, as shown (No.1).

20. Repeat 19 around scrolls on cake top.

21. Pipe lines over the suspended lines to form latticework (No.1).

22. Repeat 21 on all cake top scrolls.

23. Overpipe each scroll (No.1).

24. Picture showing completed latticework.

25. Mark a curved guide line on each side of the cake, as shown (No.1).

26. Pipe suspended lines from the guide line to the rope (No.1).

27. Pipe horizontal lines over the suspended lines to form latticework (No.1).

28. Pipe shells around each latticework (No.2).

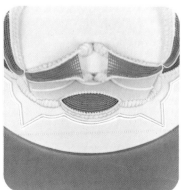

29. Pipe a line on the board, as shown (No.2); then beside the No.2 line (No.1); then overpipe the No.2 line (No.1).

30. Pipe a line on the board beside the No.1 line (No.1).

31. Fix 2 sugar bells on each top corner.

32. Fix artificial slippers, bells and ribbon, as shown.

Serena

1. Drawing showing template of heart.

2. Marzipan and coat 12″, 9″, 6″ and 4″ cakes. Place the 12″ cake on a 16″ board and then coat the board.

3. Place a 9″ cake-card on top of the 12″ cake, as shown.

4. Place the 9″ cake on the 9″ cake-card.

5. Place a 6″ cake-card on top of the 9″ cake, as shown.

6. Place the 6″ cake on the 6″ cake-card.

7. Place a 4″ cake-card on top of the 6″ cake, as shown.

8. Place the 4″ cake on the 4″ cake-card.

9. Outline heart on waxed paper (No.1).

10. Flood-in heart (L.D. 24 hrs) (80 required).

11. Pipe 120 assorted roses and rosebuds (No.57) (L.D. 24 hrs).

12. Upturn two runout hearts and join together with a 5″ length of ribbon.

13. Fix a further heart over each of the hearts in 12 (L.D. 12 hrs) (16 sets required).

14. Pipe a line around each cake-base (No. 43).

15. Pipe 'S' lines around each cake base (No.42).

16. Overpipe each 'S' line (No.2).

NOTE: *Before attempting to decorate this cake, please study the whole sequence of photographs and notes and ensure you have the proper equipment and materials, as well as sufficient time. Additional information can be found on pages 4-14 and 96.*

17. Overpipe each 'S' line (No.1).

18. Overpipe each 'S' line (No.1).

19. Pipe curved ropes around each cake-side (No.1).

20. Pipe curved ropes beside each cake-base 'S' line, as shown (No.1).

21. Picture showing cake so far.

22. Fix a set of hearts to the bottom tier cake-top edge.

23. Fix fern to ribbon.

24. Fix piped roses to fern, as shown.

25. Fix a further rose and buds, as shown, to form spray.

26. Repeat 22-25 around cakes, as indicated.

27. Place ornament on cake-top and decorate with heart sets, roses, rosebuds and fern, as required.

28. Pipe loops between each spray (No.2).

29. Pipe curved lines around cake-board edge (No.2).

30. Fix artificial horseshoes to each cake-side quarter.

31. Fix fern and roses to each cake-board quarter.

32. Fix further roses, rosebuds and a heart to complete each cake-board spray.

1. Drawing showing template of cake-top corner runout.

2. Drawing showing template of cake-base corner runout.

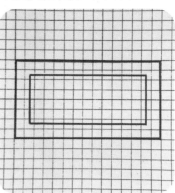

3. Drawing showing template of cake-side base runout.

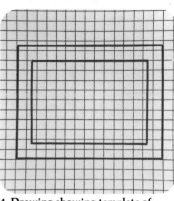

4. Drawing showing template of cake-side top runout.

5. Outline on waxed paper the cake-top corner runout (No.1).

6. Flood-in the cake-top corner runout (L.D. 24 hrs) (4 required).

7. Outline on waxed paper the cake-base corner runout (No.1).

8. Flood-in the cake-base corner runout (L.D. 24 hrs) (4 required).

9. Outline on waxed paper the cake-side base runout (No.1).

10. Flood-in the cake-side base runout.

11. Immediately fix over a 1″ diameter rod (L.D. 24 hrs) (4 cake-side base and 4 cake-side top runouts required).

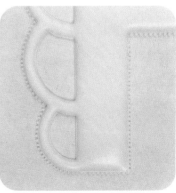

12. Pipe single dots around the edge of each cake-top corner runout (No.1).

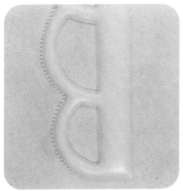

13. Pipe single dots along the outer edge of the cake-base corner runouts (No.1).

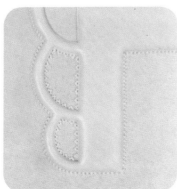

14. Pipe dots, as shown, in each of the corner runout outer apertures (No.1).

15. Pipe filigree in the centre aperture of each corner runout (No.1) (L.D. 12 hrs).

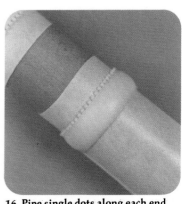

16. Pipe single dots along each end of each cake-side runout (No.1).

NOTE: *Before attempting to decorate this cake, please study the whole sequence of photographs and notes and ensure you have the proper equipment and materials, as well as sufficient time. Additional information can be found on pages 4-14 and 96.*

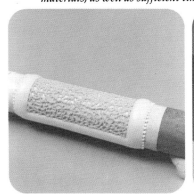

17. Pipe filigree in the centre of each cake-side runout (No.1) (L.D. 12 hrs).

18. Pipe a line at each cake-base corner (No.3) then overpipe each No.3 line (No.2) (L.D. 30m).

19. Fix cake-base corner runouts, as shown.

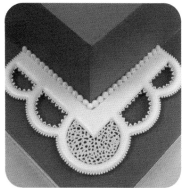

20. Pipe bulbs along the inner edge of each cake-base corner runout (No.2).

21. Pipe shells around remaining parts of cake-base (No.3).

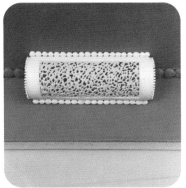

22. Fix cake-side base runouts and pipe shells, along each side of each runout (No.2).

23. Fix cake-top corner runouts.

24. Pipe shells along each cake-top edge, as shown (No.3).

25. Fix cake-side top runouts and pipe shells along each side of each runout (No.2).

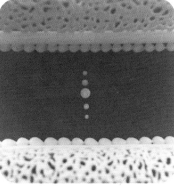

26. Pipe graduated dots between each pair of cake-side runouts (No.1).

27. Pipe pear shapes beside the graduated dots, as shown (No.1).

28. Fix artificial decorations of choice to each cake-base corner.

29. Fix artificial decorations of choice to cake-top centre.

30. Pipe pear shapes and graduated dots at cake-top centre (No.1).

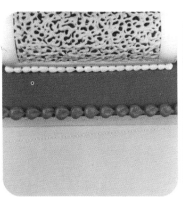

31. Pipe shells around cake-board edge (No.2).

32. Pipe a line over each cake-board edge shell (No.1).

1. Drawing showing template of letter 'K'.

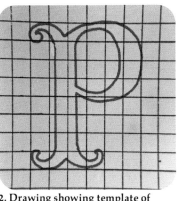

2. Drawing showing template of letter 'P'.

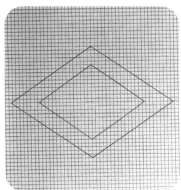

3. Drawing showing diamond template.

4. Picture showing cake scraper required.

5. Use scraper when coating cake-sides to obtain the pattern shown.

6. Outline and flood-in on waxed paper the letter 'K' (L.D. 24 hrs).

7. Outline and flood-in on waxed paper the letter 'P' (L.D. 24 hrs).

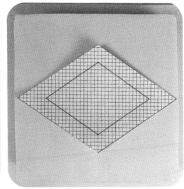

8. Cut out the diamond template shown and place on cake-top.

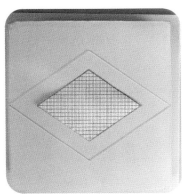

9. Pipe a line beside the diamond template (No.1) and then cut down the diamond template, as shown.

10. Pipe a line beside the diamond template (No.1).

11. Pipe two parallel lines outside each No.1 line (No.2).

12. Pipe a line outside each diamond (No.1).

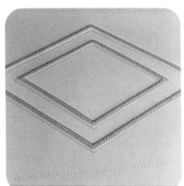

13. Pipe bulbs between each diamond No.2 lines (No.1).

14. Pipe a curved line on cake-top corner (No.3).

15. Pipe a further curved line, as shown (No.3).

16. Pipe a further curved line, as shown (No.3).

NOTE: *Before attempting to decorate this cake, please study the whole sequence of photographs and notes and ensure you have the proper equipment and materials, as well as sufficient time. Additional information can be found on pages 4-14 and 96.*

17. Repeat 14–16 at each cake-top corner.

18. Overpipe each inner curved line (No.2).

19. Pipe shells against the curved lines shown (No.2).

20. Overpipe each inner curved line (No.1) and then pipe a line over the outer shells (No.1).

21. Pipe shells along each cake-top edge corner, as shown (No.2).

22. Pipe shells around cake-base (No.3).

23. Decorate letter 'K', as shown (No.1).

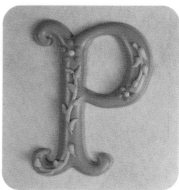

24. Decorate letter 'P', as shown (No.1).

25. Fix letters 'K' and 'P' on cake-top in position shown.

26. Fix a horseshoe and pipe the pattern shown (No.1) on opposite sides of cake-top.

27. Pipe six-dot floral pattern along cake-side band, as shown (No.1) (T).

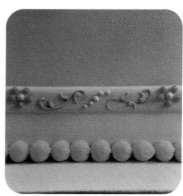

28. Complete cake-side band floral motif, as shown (No.1) (T).

29. Pipe angled lines around the cake-board in the sequence shown in picture No.12 (No.2 and No.1).

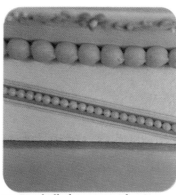

30. Pipe bulbs between each pair of cake-board No.2 lines (No.1).

31. Fix a horseshoe and pipe the pattern shown (No.1) on each cake-board corner.

32. Fix a pair of bells at each cake-base side.

NOTE: *Before attempting to decorate this cake, please study the whole sequence of photographs and notes and ensure you have the proper equipment and materials, as well as sufficient time. Additional information can be found on pages 4-14 and 96.*

About 80 roses and buds of various sizes required – see instructions.

1. 10″ round cake, 13″ round cake board and 16″ round cake board required. Mount as shown and coat in normal way.

2. Place an 8″ round cake card centrally on cake top.

3. Place an 8″ round cake on the cake card.

4. Place a 6″ cake card centrally on cake top.

5. Place a 6″ round cake on the cake card.

6. Pipe icing into the spaces between cakes (No.4). Fix a gold band to each board edge.

7. Fix 4 roses to base of cake.

8. Trail off to the left of the cake with more roses.

9. Offset sets of roses on each step.

10. Fill in space on side of bottom tier with roses.

11. Fill in space on side of middle tier with roses.

12. Fill in space on side of top tier with roses.

13. Shape and place a bulb of sugar paste in the centre of the top tier.

14. Fix a large rose to the top of the bulb.

15. Arrange and fix various sized roses around top tier edge.

16. Fix roses to the top tier to completely cover the bulb.

17. Fix artificial leaves amongst the roses on the bottom and middle tiers.

18. Fix artificial leaves amongst the roses on the side of the top tier.

19. Fix artificial leaves amongst the roses on top of the cake.

20. Fix a spray of roses and artificial leaves, as shown, on each tier at the back of the cake.

21. Pipe small bulbs around the base of each tier and around the edge of the 13″ cake board (No.3).

22. Pipe bulbs around the edges of the bottom and middle tiers (No.4) (L.D. 4 hrs).

23. Pipe a loop from the 3rd bulb to the 5th bulb (No.2) (L.D. 10 m).

24. Pipe a loop from the 2nd bulb to the 4th bulb (No.2).

25. Pipe a loop from the 4th bulb to the 6th bulb (No.2) (L.D. 10 m).

26. Pipe a loop from the 1st bulb to the 4th bulb (No.2).

27. Pipe a loop from the 4th to the 7th bulb (No.2).

28. Repeat the pattern described in 23–27 around the top edges of the bottom and middle tiers.

29. Repeat the pattern described in 23–27 against the top edge of the top tier.

30. Pipe a series of curved lines on the 16″ board (No.2).

31. Pipe a series of curved lines on the 13″ board (No.2). (Parallel to 30) as shown.

32. Repeat 31 on the top of both the bottom and middle tiers (No.2).

Trevor

NOTE: *Before attempting to decorate this cake, please study the whole sequence of photographs and notes and ensure you have the proper equipment and materials, as well as sufficient time. Additional information can be found on pages 4-14 and 96.*

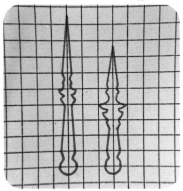

1. Drawing showing template of clock hands.

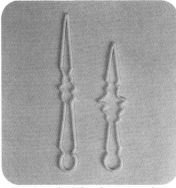

2. Outline clock hands on waxed paper (No.1).

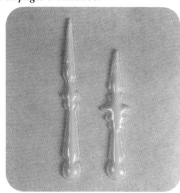

3. Flood-in clock hands (L.D. 24 hrs).

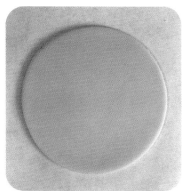

4. Roll out and cut a 4″ diameter sugar paste disc (to form clock face) (L.D. 2 hrs).

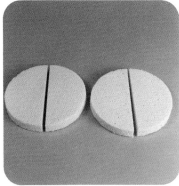

5. Cut in half two 9″ diameter × 1″ thick sponge cakes.

6. Layer sponge cakes together with jam and cream.

7. Place sponge cakes upright and cut to form clock case.

8. Use sponge cake trimmings to lengthen each end of the clock case.

9. Place sponge cake on a cake card cut to size and then cream all over.

10. Roll out, cut and fix a sheet of sugar paste over clock case top.

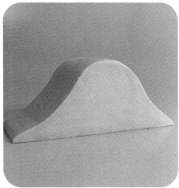

11. Roll out, cut and fix a sheet of sugar paste to each side of the clock case.

12. Picture showing first step in clock edge design. Pipe 2 bulbs on ceramic tile (No.2).

13. Picture showing next step in clock edge design. Pipe a barrel scroll (No.42).

14. Picture showing continuation of design. (Note: 12 and 13 to be repeated).

15. Place clock case on cake board and pipe the design along the front top edge of clock case.

16. Pipe the design along the back top edge of the clock case.

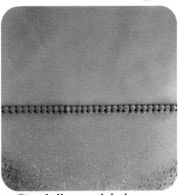

17. Pipe shells around clock case base (No.2).

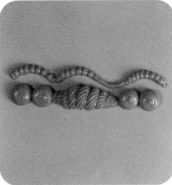

18. Pipe a curved rope beside each pair of bulbs on the tile and an 'S' scroll beside the barrel scroll (No.2).

19. Pipe a sequence of dots and a 'C' line beside the end of each barrel scroll (No.1).

20. Pipe the design over the clock case, as shown.

21. Pipe a series of scalloped ropes and dots at each end of the clock case (No.2).

22. Pipe shells around edge of clock face (No.2).

23. Pipe a line over each clock face shell (No.1).

24. Pipe numerals around clock face (No.1) (L.D. 24 hrs).

25. Fix clock face to clock case.

26. Fix hands to clock face.

27. Pipe curved lines on clock case, as shown (No.2).

28. Overpipe the curved lines (No.2).

29. Pipe the design shown down each side of the clock case (No.2).

30. Roll out, cut and place a sugar paste plaque on cake board.

31. Pipe message of choice on to plaque (No.1) and then over pipe message (No.1).

32. Pipe shells around the plaque (No.2).

1. Drawing showing template of Peter.

2. Pipe-in on waxed paper the parts shown (L.D. 20 m).

3. Pipe-in the further parts shown (L.D. 20 m).

4. Pipe-in the further parts shown (L.D. 20 m).

5. Pipe-in the further parts shown (L.D. 20 m).

6. Pipe-in the further parts shown to complete Peter (L.D. 20 m).

7. Pipe a line and dot to form fishing rod, as shown (No.2) (L.D. 24 hrs).

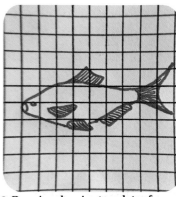

8. Drawing showing template of fish.

9. Pipe-in on waxed paper the parts of the fish shown (L.D. 20 m).

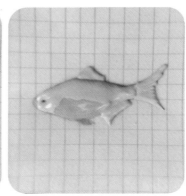

10. Pipe-in the further parts shown (L.D. 20 m).

11. Pipe-in the further parts shown to complete fish (L.D. 24 hrs). Remove waxed paper, upturn repeat 9–11.

12. Paint fish, as shown, with edible colouring (18 whole fish required).

13. Repeat 9–12 but leave a gap, as shown (3 required).

14. Remove Peter and rod from waxed paper, upturn and then repeat 2–7.

15. Picture showing coated square cake.

16. Cover the areas shown in Royal Icing to form river banks.

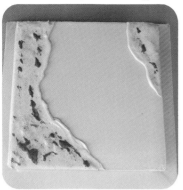

17. Stipple-in coloured Royal Icing to form ground effect.

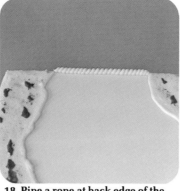

18. Pipe a rope at back edge of the cake to represent a weir (No.43).

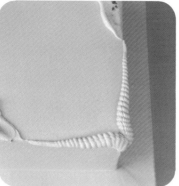

19. Pipe scrolls at the front corner of the cake to represent a waterfall (No.43).

20. Pipe a rope around the base of the cake (No.43).

21. Pipe plain shells along the parts of the cake-top edge shown (No.4).

22. Fix 2 whole fish and all heads and bodies to river, as shown.

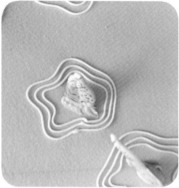

23. Pipe water ripples around each fish, as shown (No.1).

24. Fix Peter, as shown.

25. Fix the rod and then pipe a line, as shown (No.1).

26. Fix 4 whole fish in the positions shown to each side of the cake.

27. Pipe ripples and bubbles on each cake side (No.1).

28. Pipe ripples on the cake board (No.1).

29. Pipe message of choice on the cake board (No.2).

30. Overpipe the message (No.1).

31. Make 4 sugar paste fishing basket sets, as shown.

32. Fix a basket to each cake-board corner, decorate as shown (No.1) and fix ribbon to board edge.

Pamela

1. Drawing showing template of lovebirds.

2. Dawing showing template of left facing cake-side lovebird.

3. Drawing showing template of right facing cake-side lovebird.

4. Marzipan and coat a 12″ cake on a 15″ board, as shown, then coat board.

5. Marzipan and coat a 6″ heart-shape cake on a 10″ board.

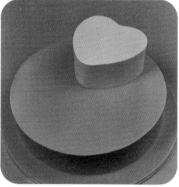

6. When dry mount heart-shape cake onto round cake in position shown.

7. Outline and flood-in on waxed paper the part of the arrow shown.

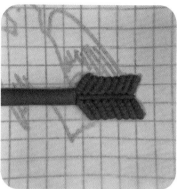

8. Pipe a central line (No.2) then pipe rope lines each side of the central line (No.1) to complete arrow (L.D. 24 hrs).

9. Pipe parts of the lovebird shown on another piece of waxed paper (No.1).

10. Pipe-in remaining parts of lovebird (L.D. 24 hrs).

11. Pipe parts of the lovebird shown on another piece of waxed paper (No.1).

12. Pipe-in remaining parts of the lovebird shown (L.D. 24 hrs).

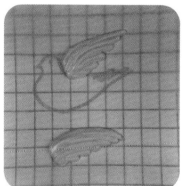

13. Pipe on waxed paper the wings of the love-bird shown (No.1) (L.D. 12 hrs) (4 left and 4 right facing lovebirds required).

14. Remove separate wing and pipe-in remaining part of one lovebird.

15. Immediately fix separate wing in position shown (L.D. 12 hrs) Repeat 14-15 for each cake-side lovebird).

16. Fix the lovebirds and arrow to cake-top, as shown.

NOTE: *Before attempting to decorate this cake, please study the whole sequence of photographs and notes and ensure you have the proper equipment and materials, as well as sufficient time. Additional information can be found on pages 4-14 and 96.*

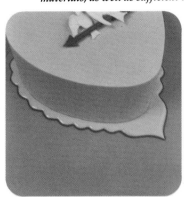

17. Outline and flood-in around base of heart shape cake, as shown (No.2) (L.D. 2 hrs).

18. Pipe shells around heart-shape cake-base (No.2).

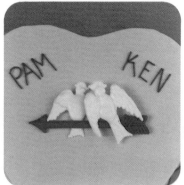

19. Pipe names of choice to heart-shape cake-top (No.1) then overpipe names (No.1).

20. Pipe a scalloped line around the heart-shape cake-top edge (No.1) then pipe dots, as shown (No.1).

21. Fix artificial flowers of choice, then pipe curved lines and dots to heart-shape cake-top (No.1).

22. Pipe a line over each cake-base shell (No.1).

23. Fix a pair of facing lovebirds to each cake-side quarter.

24. Pipe inscription of choice on cake-top, as shown (No.1) then overpipe inscription (No.1).

25. Pipe curved lines under inscription (No.1).

26. Pipe 'C' scrolls, as shown, around cake-top edge (No.3).

27. Pipe shells around cake-base (No.3).

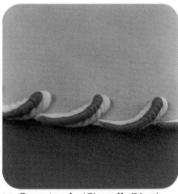

28. Overpipe the 'C' scrolls (No.2).

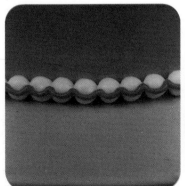

29. Pipe a line over each No.3 shell (No.2).

30. Overpipe each 'C' scroll (No.1) then overpipe each cake-base No.2 line (No.1).

31. Fix artificial matching flowers between each pair of cake-side lovebirds, then decorate, as shown (No.1).

32. Pipe curved lines around cake-board, as shown (No.1).

NOTE: *Before attempting to decorate this cake, please study the whole sequence of photographs and notes and ensure you have the proper equipment and materials, as well as sufficient time. Additional information can be found on pages 4–14 and 96.*

1. Drawing showing template of swan's body.

2. Drawing showing template of swan's wing.

3. Outline and flood-in on waxed paper 6 swan's bodies (L.D. 24 hrs).

4. Pipe on waxed paper the part of the wing shown (No.3).

5. Pipe-in the remaining wing sections (No.3).

6. Repeat 3–5 in opposite direction.

7. Whilst wet, place wings over a dowel or tube 1″ in diameter (L.D. 24 hrs) (6 of each wing required).

8. Outline and flood-in 6×1¼″ high heart plaques on waxed paper (L.D. 24 hrs).

9. Outline and flood-in – 4×2¼″ high and 4×1¾″ high – oval plaques (L.D. 24 hrs).

10. Fix swan's left and right facing bodies together and mount on the heart plaques (L.D. 2 hrs).

11. Fix wings (L.D. 2 hrs).

12. Paint beak and eyes with edible colouring.

13. Pipe scallops around the edge of each oval plaque (No.1).

14. Pipe a spike between each scallop (No.1), then pipe name of choice on each large plaque (No.1) (L.D. 12 hrs).

15. Pipe name of choice on small plaque as shown (No.1) (L.D. 12 hrs).

16. A 6″ diameter coated round cake and a 10″ square coated cake and board required.

76

17. Place 6″ thin cake board onto the square cake and mount the round cake centrally.

18. Pipe shells around the base of each cake (No.44) and fix plaques as shown.

19. Pipe shells around top edge of the round cake (No.44).

20. Pipe shells on the edge above each square cake plaque (No.44).

21. Pipe an 'S' scroll on each side of the square cake top edge shells (No.44).

22. Overpipe all base shells with a line (No.2).

23. Pipe a decorative line on each cake top corner, as shown (No.2).

24. Overpipe each scroll (No.2).

25. Pipe a line on the cake board, as shown (No.2).

26. Overpipe the round cake base No.2 line (No.1) and pipe a dot between each round cake-top shell (No.1).

27. Overpipe the square cake base No.2 line (No.1) and pipe a dot between each square cake-top shell (No.1).

28. Fix an artificial baby to the back of each of 2 swans and an artificial flower of choice to the back of each of 4 swans.

29. Pipe reins from beak to baby's hands (No.1).

30. Fix swans in the positions shown and add matching artificial flowers.

31. Pipe a 'V' line beside each corner 'V' on board (No.1).

32. Fix artificial flowers and leaves and ribbon of choice, as shown.

Courtney

1. Roll out and cut black coloured sugar paste strips to cover bottom half of each side of cake.

2. Roll out and cut white sugar paste strips to cover top half of each side of cake.

3. Roll out and leave on icing sugared table top, a thin sheet of white sugar paste the exact size of the cake top.

4. Mark and score the sheet of sugar paste into 12 equal vertical widths.

5. Mark and score the sheet of sugar paste into 12 equal horizontal widths.

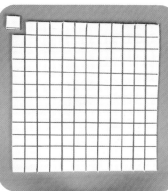

6. Cut through the scores on the sugar paste, thus obtaining 144 equally sized squares (L.D. 2 hrs).

7. Roll out a sheet of sugar paste to make 36 squares, but in black.

8. Mark, score and cut sugar paste sheet into 36 squares (L.D. 2 hrs).

9. Align and fix the first 5 squares (in the order shown) with the top left edge of the cake.

10. Finish the first line.

11. Fix squares in the order shown for the next 3 lines. (A ruler edge may be used to straighten-up the lines).

12. Fix squares in the order shown for the next 4 lines (8 lines are now completed).

13. Complete fixing the squares over the cake top in the order shown.

14. Indication of the size of numerals in comparison to size of a square.

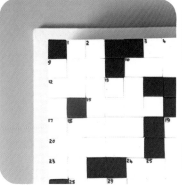

15. Pipe numerals in top left corner of cake, as shown, in black coloured Royal Icing (No.1).

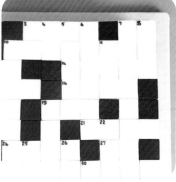

16. Pipe numerals in top right corner of cake, as shown, in black coloured Royal Icing (No.1).

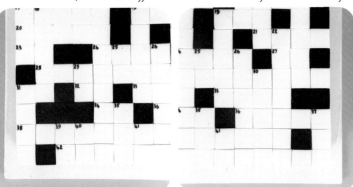

17. Pipe numerals in bottom left corner of cake, as shown, in black coloured Royal Icing (No.1).

18. Pipe numerals in bottom right corner of cake, as shown, in black coloured Royal Icing (No.1).

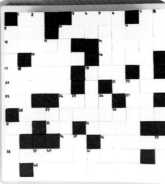

19. This photograph shows the top of the cake complete with numerals.

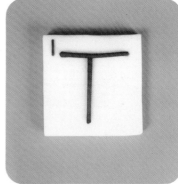

20. Indication of the size of letters in comparison to size of a square.

21. Pipe lettering, as shown, in first line (No.1).

22. Complete lettering, as shown, on cake top (No.1).

23. Roll out and cut 2 white and 2 black sugar paste strips to cover the length and width of the cake board border.

24. Mark and cut the 4 strips into 48 equal pieces.

25. Fix, as shown, 1 black piece.

26. Fix, as shown, 1 white piece.

27. Continue alternating colours to length of cake.

28. Leaving corners of board blank, repeat 27 on the 3 remaining board borders.

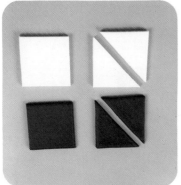

29. Mark and diagonally cut 2 black and 2 white squares to fit, each board corner, as shown.

30. Fix the triangular pieces to corners, as shown.

31. Fix artificial flowers of choice to each side of cake.

32. Fix velvet ribbon to edge of cake board.

1. 8″×8″ square cake required.

2. Cut off a 2″ slice.

3. Fix slice to end of cake and remove surplus.

4. Trim left side of cake to form book spine.

5. Marzipan and coat cake in normal way on board.

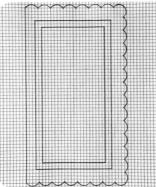

6. Drawing showing template of book cover – 11″×6¼″.

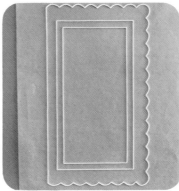

7. Outline the book cover areas shown on waxed paper (No.2).

8. Flood-in the white frame shown (L.D. 6 hrs).

9. Flood-in remaining areas in black, as shown (L.D. 24 hrs).

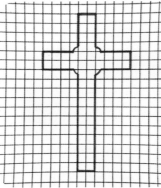

10. Drawing showing template of Cross – 3¼″ high.

11. Outline and flood-in the Cross on waxed paper (L.D. 24 hrs).

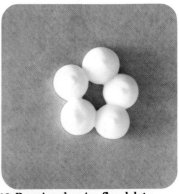

12. Drawing showing floral dot sequence to be piped on waxed paper (No.2) (L.D. 1 hr).

13. Complete the flower with a piped dot centre (No.2) (L.D. 12 hrs) (20 flowers of various sizes required).

14. Pipe shells around the Cross edges (No.2).

15. Pipe lines on the Cross, as shown (No.2) and then overpipe the No.2 lines (No.1).

16. Pipe initial of choice at centre of Cross (No.1) (L.D. 12 hrs).

17. Roll out a thin sheet of sugar paste and fix to the spine of the 'book'.

18. Coat sides of cake using a (sterilised) fine toothed comb to create a page effect (L.D. 4 hrs).

19. Pipe a curved line on the board to match the top cover template (No.2).

20. Flood-in in black between the cake base and the No.2 line.

21. Fix the Cross centrally to the top cover.

22. Pipe curved lines at the base of the Cross, as shown (No.1).

23. Fix flowers to the curved lines, as shown.

24. Pipe inscription of choice on cover (No.1).

25. Pipe 'S' pattern on the white frame, as shown (No.1).

26. Pipe dots beside each 'S' pattern, as shown (No.1).

27. Pipe curved lines on the top and bottom right-hand corners of the top cover (No.1).

28. Fix flowers to the curved lines, as shown.

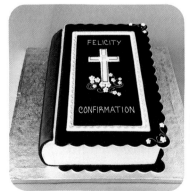

29. Fix cover to the cake.

30. Pipe rope lines to spine, as shown (No.44).

31. Pipe inscription of choice to spine (No.2).

32. Pipe a matching 'S' pattern each side of the inscription (No.2) and fix ribbon to board edge.

Andrew

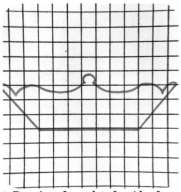

1. Drawing of template for side of CRADLE.

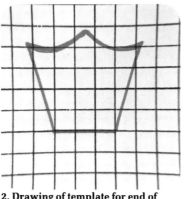

2. Drawing of template for end of CRADLE.

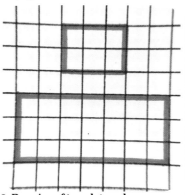

3. Drawing of templates – large oblong, CRADLE BASE and BLANKET – small oblong for PILLOW.

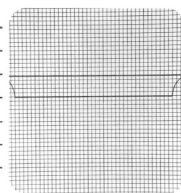

4. Drawing of template for cake top runouts.

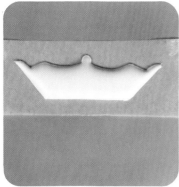

5. Outline and flood-in side of CRADLE (L.D. 24 hrs) (2 required).

6. Outline and flood-in end of CRADLE (L.D. 24 hrs) (2 required).

7. Outline and flood-in the PILLOW, CRADLE BASE and BLANKET (one of each required) (L.D. 24 hrs).

8. Outline and flood-in the cake top runout (4 required) (L.D. 24 hrs).

9. Decorate the CRADLE sides as shown (No.1).

10. Pipe a row of single dots over each CRADLE end top (No.1).

11. Pipe 6-dot sequence and decorate, as shown (No.1) (L.D. 12 hrs).

12. Fix sides and ends to CRADLE BASE.

13. Pipe small shells along inside joins and pipe a line around the top inside of the CRADLE (No.1).

14. Upturn CRADLE and pipe shells along joins. Pipe 2 lines to form rockers (No.1) (L.D. 10 m). Repeat overpiping twice (L.D. 12 hrs).

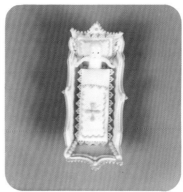

15. Fix PILLOW, baby-doll and BLANKET into CRADLE.

16. Pipe a ⅜″ diameter bulb on to waxed paper to form RATTLE (No.3) (10 required) (L.D. 2 hrs).

17. Pipe lines and a circle, as shown (No.1) (L.D. 1 hr).

18. Pipe a row of dots between the parallel lines (No.1) (L.D. 1 hr).

19. Pipe a bow on the RATTLE handle (No.1) (L.D. 12 hrs).

20. Fix and align cake top runouts (No.3).

21. Pipe a line on cake board following the cake top runout design (No.2).

22. Flood-in between the No.2 line and cake base (L.D. 12 hrs).

23. Pipe a line on the cake top ⅛″ inside the runout (No.2). Pipe a 'V' and two curves on each top runout (No.2).

24. Repeat the 'V's and curves on cake board runouts (No.2).

25. Flood-in between the top two No.2 lines and between the board No.2 line and the cake base (L.D. 12 hrs).

26. Pipe a line of bulbs around the top inside edge of runouts (No.2).

27. Pipe a line of bulbs around the cake base (No.2).

28. Pipe small dots against the No.2 line on top of all runouts (No.1).

29. Pipe names of choice on cake top (No.2).

30. Overpipe the names and lightly pipe the decorative curves (No.1).

31. Fix a pair of RATTLES and the CRADLE to the cake top and decorate with parallel lines (No.1).

32. Fix pairs of RATTLES to cake sides, artificial leaves, flowers to corners and ribbon to board.

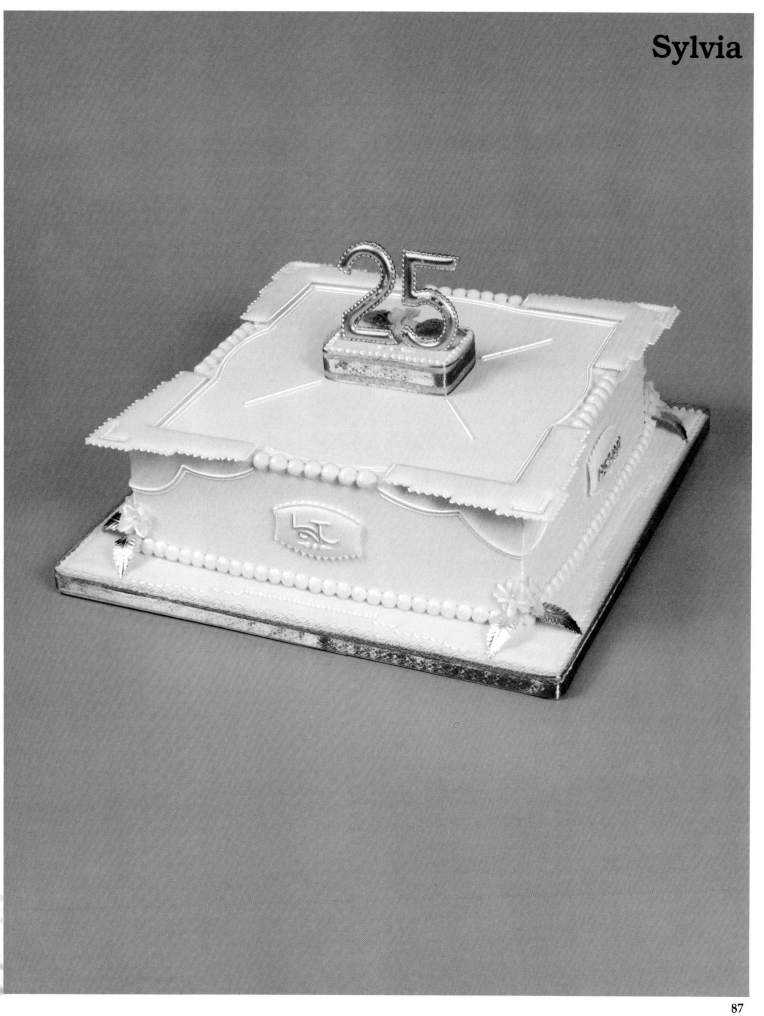

NOTE: Before attempting to decorate this cake, please study the whole sequence of photographs and notes and ensure you have the proper equipment and materials, as well as sufficient time. Additional information can be found on pages 4-14 and 96.

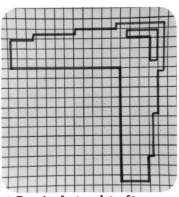

1. Drawing for template of top corner runout (4 required).

2. Using template under waxed paper outline corner runouts (No.1).

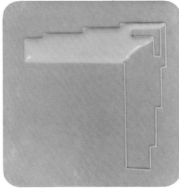

3. Flood-in corner runouts (L.D. 24 hrs).

4. Pipe 6-dot sequence, single dots and filigree, as shown (No.1) (L.D. 12 hrs).

5. Drawing for template of '25'.

6. Using template under waxed paper outline the obverse and reverse of the '25' (No.1).

7. Flood-in the '25' (L.D. 24 hrs).

8. Fix each pair of numerals together. Pipe shells around edges (No.1) (L.D. 12 hrs).

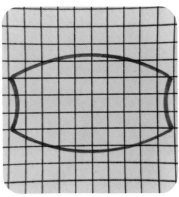

9. Drawing for template of plaque (4 required).

10. Using template under waxed paper outline plaque (No.1).

11. Flood-in plaque. Repeat 10 and 11 for each plaque. (L.D. 24 hrs).

12. Pipe 6-dot sequence and single dots, as shown (No.1) (L.D. 12 hrs).

13. Pipe a line (the length of the runout) on each corner (No.3) (L.D. 2 hrs).

14. Overpipe the No.3 lines (No.2).

15. Immediately fix and align the corner runouts (L.D. 30 m).

16. Pipe small bulbs between runouts and cake top (No.2) (T).

17. Following runout design, pipe a line on cake board (No.2).

18. Flood-in board between the No.2 line and cake base (L.D. 12 hrs).

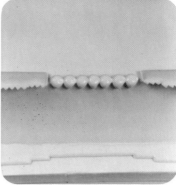

19. Pipe plain shells between corner runouts on top edge of cake (No.3).

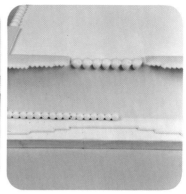

20. Pipe small plain shells around cake base (No.3).

21. Pipe straight corner lines and then pipe curved lines between runouts (No.2).

22. Pipe 2 curved lines under each corner runout on sides of cake (No.2) (T).

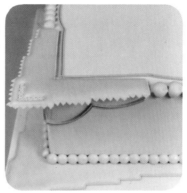

23. Pipe a line beside all No.2 lines, then overpipe all No.2 lines (No.1) (T as necessary).

24. Pipe 6-dot sequence around cake board corner runouts (No.1).

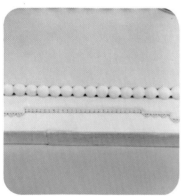

25. Pipe plain shells along each board runout side (No.1).

26. Cut a block of sugar paste 3″ long, 1¾″ wide and 1″ deep (L.D. 2 hrs).

27. Pipe initials of choice on plaque (No.1) and decorate as shown (No.1) (L.D. 2 hrs).

28. Paint '25'. Fix onto block. Pipe shells around top edge (No.1).

29. Fix ribbon around block and decorate with artificial flowers and leaves.

30. Place '25' centrally on cake and pipe 4 diagonal lines (No.2).

31. Pipe a shorter line each side of each diagonal line (No.1) and overpipe each diagonal No.2 line (No.1).

32. Fix plaques to cake sides, artificial flowers and leaves at base corners.

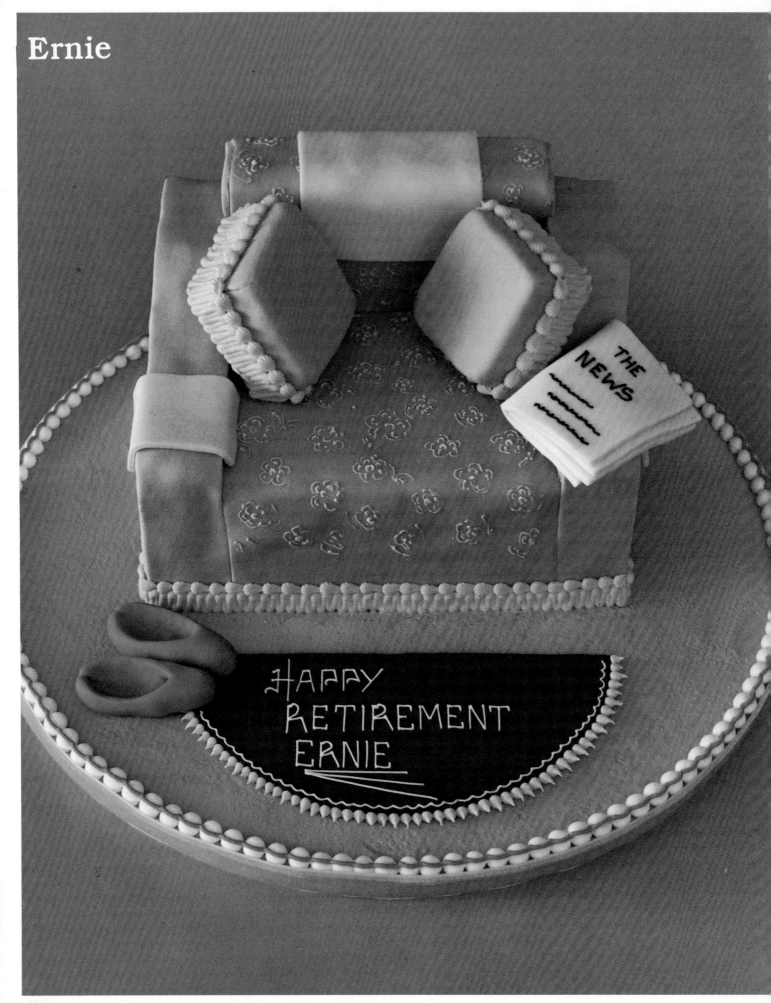

NOTE: Before attempting to decorate this cake, please study the whole sequence of photographs and notes and ensure you have the proper equipment and materials, as well as sufficient time. Additional information can be found on pages 4-14 and 96.

1. One sponge cake – 6″×8″×1″ – required for the chair arms.

2. Two sponge cakes – each 5″×4″×1″ – required for the seat.

3. One sponge cake – 5″×5″×1″ – required for the chair back.

4. Two sponge cakes – each 2″×2″×1″ – required for cushions.

5. Cut 'arms' sponge in shaped half, as shown.

6. Jam and cream the seat sponges together.

7. Fix the chair back to the seat with jam and cream.

8. Fix the arms in position with jam and cream.

9. Place the chair on a 14″ round cake board and cover with cream.

10. Roll out, cut and place a sugar paste cover over the seat and back, as shown.

11. Roll out, cut and place sugar paste covers over the inside and outside of the arms.

12. Roll out, cut and place sugar paste covers over the remaining areas.

13. Roll out, cut and place sugar paste covers over the two cushions, fixing with cream.

14. Picture showing antique floral design for chair covering.

15. Pipe floral design over the area shown (No.1).

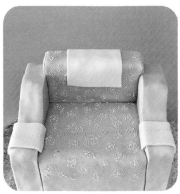

16. Roll out, cut and place sugar paste chair covers, as shown.

91

NOTE: Before attempting to decorate this cake, please study the whole sequence of photographs and notes and ensure you have the proper equipment and materials, as well as sufficient time. Additional information can be found on pages 4-14 and 96.

17. Stipple the board with Royal Icing to create carpet effect.

18. Roll out, cut and place sugar paste mat on board.

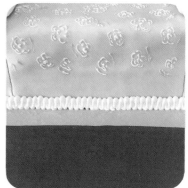

19. Pipe fringe around chair base (No.42).

20. Pipe shells above the fringe (No.42).

21. Pipe fringe around the base of each cushion (No.42).

22. Pipe shells above each cushion fringe (No.42).

23. Pipe spikes around the curved edge of the mat (No.42).

24. Roll out and cut two pieces of sugar paste – each 2″×3½″.

25. Place the two pieces together and fold to form newspaper.

26. Pipe wording and imitation print on the newspaper (No.1).

27. Form a pair of slippers from sugar paste.

28. Position cushions, newspaper and slippers.

29. Pipe message of choice on the mat (No.1).

30. Pipe lines under message and scallops around mat, as shown (No.1).

31. Pipe shells around top edge of cake board (No.3).

32. Overpipe the board shells with a line (No.1) and fix ribbon to board edge.

The cake reads: "Congratulations on your Engagement Claire and Robert"

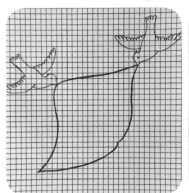

1. Drawing showing template of doves and plaque.

2. Pipe the right wing of the left dove on waxed paper (and keep separate from remainder of dove) (No.1) (L.D. 12 hrs).

3. Pipe the left wing of the right dove on waxed paper (and keep separate from remainder of dove) (No.1) (L.D. 12 hrs).

4. Pipe the left wing of the left dove on waxed paper (No.1).

5. Pipe the head, body and tail of the left dove against the left wing (No.1) (L.D. 24 hrs).

6. Pipe the right wing of the right dove on waxed paper (No.1).

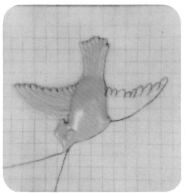

7. Pipe the head, body and tail of the right dove against the right wing (No.1) (L.D. 24 hrs).

8. Outline and flood-in the plaque on waxed paper (L.D. 24 hrs).

9. Drawing showing template of love-birds (6 love-birds required).

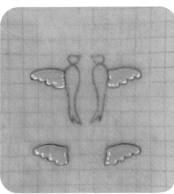

10. Pipe-in the wings on waxed paper, as shown (No.1) (L.D. 12 hrs).

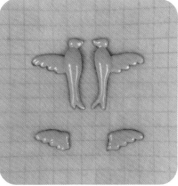

11. Pipe-in heads and bodies on waxed paper, as shown (No.1).

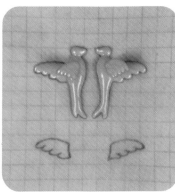

12. Remove love-bird loose wings and fix to bodies, as shown (L.D. 12 hrs).

13. Fix loose doves' wings to bodies at the angle shown (support as necessary) (L.D. 12 hrs).

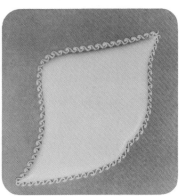

14. Pipe 'S' scrolls around the edge of the plaque (No.1).

15. Pipe a line along the inside edge of the plaque and pipe sequences of dots to form floral design (No.1).

16. Pipe message of choice in 'flow' of plaque (No.1) (L.D. 12 hrs).

94

17. Drawing showing template of heart-shape plaques.

18. Outline and flood-in hearts on waxed paper (L.D. 24 hrs). (6 hearts required).

19. Pipe dots around the edge of each heart (No.1).

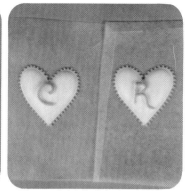

20. Pipe an initial of choice on each heart (No.1)(L.D. 12 hrs).

21. Pipe shells around top edge and base of cake (No.44).

22. Finish front of base with a long shell (No.44).

23. Overpipe each top shell with a heart design (No.3).

24. Overpipe each base shell with a heart design (No.3).

25. Overpipe each No.3 design (No.2).

26. Overpipe each No.2 design (No.1).

27. Fix plaque and doves to cake top.

28. Fix hearts and supporting love-birds to the front and each side of cake, as shown.

29. Fix artificial flowers and decorations of choice, as shown.

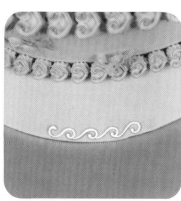

30. Pipe 'S' scrolls around cake board edge (No.2).

31. Pipe floral dot sequences between each board scroll (No.1).

32. Fix decorative ribbon to board edge.

Index/Glossary.